SCOTLAND'S
CASTLES

SCOTLAND'S CASTLES

RESCUED, REBUILT AND REOCCUPIED

JANET BRENNAN-INGLIS

Dedicated to the memory of
Professor Charles McKean,
a kind and generous scholar

First published 2014

The History Press
The Mill, Brimscombe Port
Stroud, Gloucestershire, GL5 2QG
www.thehistorypress.co.uk

British Library Cataloguing in Publication Data.
A catalogue record for this book is available from the British Library.

ISBN 978 0 7509 5445 7

Typesetting and origination by The History Press
Printed in Great Britain

CONTENTS

ABOUT THE AUTHOR

Dr Janet Brennan-Inglis bought Barholm Castle in Galloway in 1999, along with her husband John, and they began the long process of restoring it from a ruined shell surrounded by thistles and hogweed to a comfortable home with a beautiful garden. Since completing the restoration in 2006 Janet has been researching and photographing the other restored castles of Scotland, and also those that are still ruined and in need of rescue before it is too late. She was awarded a doctorate for her research in 2011.

Janet is a lecturer for NADFAS and lectures on Scottish castles and heritage throughout the UK. She is Chair of the Scottish Castles Association, secretary of the National Trust for Scotland Galloway Members Group, special interest organiser for NADFAS south-west Scotland branch, county organiser of Scotland's Gardens and is an active member of the Galloway Preservation Society.

ACKNOWLEDGEMENTS

For proofreading, helpful suggestions and general support, my grateful thanks go to: Dr John Brennan, my dear husband and partner in the restoration of Barholm Castle; Alastair Bain, treasurer of the SCA; John Buchanan-Smith, owner of Newmilns Tower; Michael Davis, historian and author; Dr David and Janet Hannay, stewards of Sorbie Castle; Dr John and Hazel Hunter, owners of Ochiltree Castle; Brian McGarrigle, council member of SCA. Heartfelt thanks to the many castle owners and restorers who have welcomed me to their homes, allowing me to take photographs with access to private spaces, and answering endless questions. All images are the author's own unless credited otherwise.

For generous assistance with information, visits, photographs, etc., I am indebted to: Geoffrey and Venetia Anderson, owners and restorers of Lochnaw Castle; Sue and Steve Atterton, owners of Ravenstone Castle; Ann and Anthony Bartleet, owners of Craigcaffie Castle; David Bertie, owner of the Old Place of Mochrum; Sue and Ian Brash, owners of Fa'side Castle; Andrew Briggs, artist; James Brown, owner of Baltersan; Jeffrey and Janet Burn, owners and restorers of Buittle Tower; Buffy Carson and her late husband, Graham, restorers of Rusco Tower; Robert Clow, restorer of Aiket Castle, and editor of *Restoring Scotland's Castles*, a source of much material; Dr John and Kay Coyne, owners and restorers of Tilquhillie Castle; Fay Cowan, owner and restorer of Glenapp Castle; Marybelle Drummond, daughter-in-law of the Earl of Perth, who restored Stobhall Castle; Mark Ellington, owner and restorer of Towie Barclay; Gavin Farquharson, owner of Ecclesgreig Castle; Agatha Ann Graves, historian of Castle Wigg; Nicholas Groves-Raines, architect and restorer of Liberton House; George and Ann Jamieson, owners and restorers of Cramond Tower; Peter and Lesley Kormylo, restorers of Abbot's Tower; Sandy and Moira Leask, owners and restorers of Old Sauchie; Phill Levey, owner and builder of Craigietocher; Mats Ljungberg, photographer; John and Mary McMurtrie, owners of Balbithan; Roger Masterton at Celtic Castles; Richard Paxman, aka 'Arjayempee' on Flickr, castle photographer; Lachlan Rhodes, restorer of Terpersie Castle; Andy Ritchie, owner of Brackenhill and Lochhouse towers; Lady Steel, restorer of Aikwood Tower; Simpson and Brown Architects, for permission to reprint drawings; Frans Smoor, architect and restorer of Gagie House; Leith and Rachel Stuart, owners of Blackhall Manor; Paul and Josine Veenhuijzen, owners of Earlshall Castle.

CASTLE RESTORATION CONTRIBUTORS

The architects, artists, authors, campaigners, organisations,
owners and restorers who feature in this book:

Al-Fayed, Mohammed
Allward, Stewart
Atterton, Sue and Steve
Bailey, Helen
Balgonie, Laird and Younger
Banister, John
Begg, Ian
Binney, Marcus
Boswell, Harry
Brash, Ian
Brennan, John and Janet
Briggs, Andrew
Brown, James
Browne, Nicholas
Bryce, David
Buchanan-Smith, John
Burn, Jeffrey and Janet
Burn, William
Carson, Buffy and Graham
Charles, Prince of Wales
Clarke, George
Clarke, Peter and Gillian
Clarke, Tom and Olive
Clow, Robert
Cole, Stephen
Corbett, Judy
Cormack, Patrick
Cornforth, John
Cowan, Fay and Graham
Coyne, John and Kay
Davey, Andrew
Davis, Michael
De la Lanne-Mirrlees, Robin
Dewar, Bill and Ann
Dobson, Perle and Sam
Donnachie, Dave
Drummond, Peter
Ellington, Marc
Erbe, Tim
Fairbairn, Nicholas
Farquharson, Gavin

Friends of Portencross Castle
Gifford, John
Gillies, Peter
Gordon Lennox, George
Gordon, Granville (Marquis of Huntly)
Gray, Nick and Amanda
Grossart, Angus
Groves-Raines, Nicholas
Guyot, Michel
Hamlyn, Helen
Hannay, David
Harper, Alastair
Harris, John
Hewkin, Peter
Hope Dickson, Archibald
Hutton, David
Irons, Jeremy
Jamieson, Eric and George
Johnstone, David
Jokilehto, Jukka
Kelsall, Moultrie
Koerner, Lisbet
Kormylo, Peter and Lesley
Laing, Gerald
Laird, Michael
Landmark Trust
Leask, Sandy and Moira
Leslie, David
Level, Phill
Lindsay, Ian
Lindsay, Maurice
Lorimer, Patrick
Lorimer, Robert
Lumsden, David
MacDougall, Hope
MacGibbon, David
MacInnes, Ranald
Maclean, Fitzroy
Maclean-Bristol, Nicholas
Macneil, Robert
Maitland-Carew, Gerald

Marie, Queen of Romania
Martin, Kit
Maxwell-Stewart, Catherine
McKean, Charles
McMurtrie, Mary
Merredew, Jennifer
Millar, Gordon
Miller, Christian
Morris, William
Murdoch, Ken and Anna
Nairn, Richard and Malin
Newall, Walter
Nicholsby, Geoffrey
Oliphant, Roderick
Paolozzi, Eduardo
Parris, Matthew
Paterson, George
Pearson, David
Perth, David and Nancy
Plevey, Phill
Pooley, Robert
Ptolomey, Tony
Queen Elizabeth, the Queen Mother
Rasmussen, Michael
Rhodes, John
Rhodes, Lachlan
Ritchie, Andy
Ross, Thomas
Rowan, Mike
Roy, James Charles
Russell, Michael
Safdie, Moshie
Salter, Mike
Saltire Society
SAVE Britain's Heritage

Scottish Castles Association
Scottish Civic Trust
Scott-Moncrieff, George
Scott-Plummer, Alexa
Sempill-Forbes, Margaret
Shaw, Francis
Simpson, Ian
Simpson, James
Smoor, Francis
Spence, Basil
Spence, Roy
Spens, Michael
Steel, David and Judy
Stenhouse, Rosamond
Stewart, Lachlan and Annie
Strachan, Alex
Strong, Roy
Stuart, Charles and Elizabeth
Stuart, Leith and Rachel
Taylor, Robert
Thomas, William
Tranter, Nigel
Turnbull, Nigel
Tweedy Savage, Ann
Udny-Hamilton, Margaret
Vivat Trust
Walker, David
Wemyss, Charles
Wharton, Ric
Wontner, Hugh
Wood, Colin
Wood, Crichton
Yeats, William Butler
Yorke, Stephen
Ziolkowski, Theodore

CHAPTER 1

INTRODUCTION

The Iconic Castle

Is there any other building type that has the same power to attract fascination, interest and even devotion in people of all ages, cultures and classes, and the same symbolic representation of power and romance? The romantic appeal of castellated architecture can be traced in art and literature for centuries up to the present day, from Arthurian legends through Sir Walter Scott's gothic novels to the setting of the Harry Potter books in magnificent Hogwarts. Representations of the castle in novels, glossy periodicals, television programmes, the Internet, video games and films provide a window into popular culture and a reflection of

Schloss Neuschwanstein in Germany (© Thomas Wolf, www.foto-tw.de)

the excitement and fantasies that the buildings inspire. Scholars, too, find castles seductively attractive, and have even appropriated a new term to cover their field of study: 'castellology'. Of all architectural forms, the castle is surely the most written about and loved. Edinburgh Castle, in a country of only 5 million inhabitants, receives over 1 million visitors every year.

In Scotland, the castle is an iconic and idealised representation of heritage and even national identity and as such is seen as unchanging and eternal. But all is not as it seems; even the castle that most clearly epitomises Scottish historical continuity on calendars and shortbread tins, Eilean Donan, is a modern rebuild based on romantic imaginings rather than evidence, and the cause of controversy over its 'restoration' early last century.

More recently, between 1945 and 2010, around 130 Scottish castles were restored for reoccupation from a ruinous or derelict state, or brought back from the brink of dereliction with programmes of extensive repairs. There was a wide-scale renewal of Scottish castellated buildings in the second half of the twentieth century – a renaissance of Renaissance buildings, one might say. In addition to the full restorations, more than 150 castles were saved from potential decay through timely repairs and rejuvenation by new owners, and at least sixteen new tower houses were built that mimic sixteenth-century design. This occurred alongside a widening of public access, as castle owners turned increasingly to commercial activities, and many changes in ownership. Although castle restoration is not a new phenomenon – and indeed has been an ongoing activity since at least the eighteenth century – the recent number of restorations has been much greater than in any preceding period and the reasons for undertaking them have changed. Since 1945, there has been an extraordinary level of castle conservation activity for such a small country in such a short space of time. Scotland has between 1,000 and 2,000 castles still standing, depending upon how one defines a 'castle', and is very fortunate that a significant proportion of them has benefited from the current golden age of building and rebuilding. However, there is no room for complacency, as many others are in a perilous state and need rescuing from imminent decay and disaster.

This book will examine the reasons for this modern Renaissance of Scottish castles, setting the context of the social, economic and polit-ical changes that took place in the post-Second World War years and investigating the fascinating individual stories of castle owners and their resto-ration projects. I have been privileged to play a small part in this larger tale, through the restoration of Barholm Castle in Galloway (*See* Chapter 6).

But First – What is a Castle?

Or rather, what do we understand a castle to be? If one looks at some of the stereotypical features of 'castle' – old, made of stone, tall, large, turrets, crenellations, moat, drawbridge – the only common feature seems to be 'made of stone'. This is hardly sufficient to hold the whole concept together, since cottages and windmills and apartment blocks can also be made of stone, and castles are not even necessarily so – some, like the heavily fortified Potala Palace in Tibet, are even made of wood and straw. Most castles are old, but not all, and the same applies to the other defining features; there are always many exceptions. Dictionary definitions emphasise fortifications and largeness; this seems to reflect the broad understanding, which most people have, of what castles can be, i.e. buildings that look defensive but are not necessarily fortified. Definitions, though, however carefully crafted, do not necessarily represent objects, as we individually understand them. If we look at various castellated buildings, such as Schloss Neuschwanstein in Germany, upon which the symbolic Disney castle was reputedly modelled, grand country mansions and palaces like Culzean Castle in Ayrshire, and small ruined towers throughout Scotland, the main relationship that links castles of all types is a seductive historical romanticism. Fantasies are generated when people visit castles and played out when they buy them.

Some castle guidebooks take an extremely simple and direct approach: if the building is named Castle 'X' or 'X' Castle it is included, otherwise, not. On the whole, this rather crude distinction works quite well. But Abbot's Tower, Linlithgow Palace, Old Place of Mochrum, House of the Binns, Vaila Hall and Baltersan, which is always referred to as plain Baltersan, are all just as much 'castles' (or not, depending on your views about the proper nature of a castle). They just suffer from what the historian Ian Grimble calls the 'accident of nomenclature'. The small castles and tower houses of Scotland are also sometimes referred to as fortalices, keeps or peels; the grander Renaissance buildings, which owe much to French influences, feature as chateaux in Charles McKean's book, *The Scottish Chateau*, deliberately named to draw the reader

Drumlanrig Castle, which includes a sixteenth-century core, heavily remodelled in the seventeenth century (© Joergsam)

away from the notion of fortification. But, although the use of 'castle' as a catch-all descriptor of all buildings that look fortified (even if the promise of defence is a blatant impossibility) may be somewhat contentious; it is convenient if we want to avoid missing out on some very interesting buildings. In this book, the widest definition is taken, to include all buildings that are called 'castle' and/or look like a castle, from large medieval fortresses via small, sixteenth-century towers to big, Victorian castellated mansions that are blatant fakes – some of which even have the core of a genuine late-medieval tower tucked away in their palatial interiors, such as Cawdor Castle, Culzean Castle and Drumlanrig Castle.

Indeed, even among considerably older buildings, the 'castle' appellation is often not original, but a later addition: a romantic conceit added in the nineteenth century.

The heyday of castle building in Scotland was 1500–1680, when it is estimated that more than 1,000 castles were built. A second flush occurred throughout the nineteenth century, when nouveaux riches industrialists rushed to build themselves castles, aided by architects such as William Burn and David Bryce in the Gothic Revival style, and later in the Balmorial style popularised by Queen Victoria. Wealthy aristocrats disguised their outmoded but genuine late-medieval castles by refashioning them as pseudo-gothic castles, such as Kinnaird Castle in Montrose.

And What is a Restoration?

'Restoration' is also a tricky term. It is a word bandied about imprecisely when applied to buildings, covering activity across the spectrum from extensive interior redecoration to complete rebuilding; it is also a word, like its close associate, 'heritage', heavy with significance (both positive and negative) for those with strong views on architecture. The Scottish Castles Association (SCA) was founded in 1996, and represents many of the restoring owners and new owners of smaller towers and castles. The body lists the following as one of its objectives: 'Encouraging the responsible ownership, conservation and restoration of ruined structures, and other buildings at risk, in the belief that, in many cases, restoration offers the best means of ensuring their long-term survival.' The media tend to be supportive of this view, with many admiring television programmes and articles in glossy magazines and newspapers that praise the courage, foresight, determination and good taste of restorers. But, not everyone agrees.

William Morris, Victorian Pre-Raphaelite artist, craftsman and political campaigner, set up the Society for the Protection of Ancient Buildings (SPAB) in 1877. SPAB's manifesto was a purist plea:

... to resist all tampering with either the fabric or ornament of the building as it stands; if it has become inconvenient for its present use, to raise another building rather than alter or enlarge the old one; in fine to treat our ancient buildings as monuments of a bygone art, created by bygone manners, that modern art cannot meddle with without destroying.

SPAB's preservationist campaigning carried on throughout the twentieth century, with members still today required to sign up to the manifesto. It has always been a very small player in the field of heritage organisations, and only acquired a separate Scottish branch in 1995. However, its long-term influence on conservationists in the architectural profession – although difficult to measure – has doubtless been significant and has led to disputes between purists and pragmatists.

I have used the term 'restoration' mainly to apply to the rebuilding and reoccupation of properties that were uninhabited and uninhabitable, ranging from roofless ruins to recently derelict buildings, although a few dilapidated and almost deserted castles, such as Cleish and Buittle Tower, have crept in if they are especially interesting. Restoration does not mean that the past has been faithfully recreated, even if this is implied. It is simply not possible to pour the past back into a building. However, most restoration projects have at least tried to be faithful to the past and aimed for authenticity, filling the rooms with period furniture and reclaimed building materials, although some have got much closer than others.

Courtesy of
Richard Paxman

So, when numbers are bandied about in this book referring to Scottish castles and their restorations, be aware that these are viewed through the prism of my very personal take on what constitutes a castle and what it means to restore one. Every restoration project has a back-story and most narratives come with themes of derring-do, heroic endeavour and romantic obsession. Restorers took gigantic risks and battled horrible odds as they spent years sleeping in freezing caravans in the grounds of their ruined castles, begging for money from banks charging 17.5 per cent interest rates and despairing of ever completing the work they had started. Yet well over 100 of them succeeded and several more are still going through the processes of bringing back a ruin from the brink of disaster.

Moreover, around 150 more were brought back from the very brink of ruin by programmes of intensive repairs. If we count the total conservatively as 275 castles that have been rescued (125 restored and 150 heavily repaired) since 1945, that really is a huge number for a very small country in a very short space of time, representing somewhere between 15–30 per cent of all castles, depending on the definition. The second half of the twentieth century saw a Golden Age of castle and tower house restoration in Scotland, with a far greater level of castle-related building activity than at any time since the sixteenth century. Sadly, significant numbers of Scottish castles were lost early in this same period, through demolition, fire and fatal neglect (*See* Chapter 7).

At Thirlestane Castle in the Borders, for example, the rot was literally stopped. When Captain Gerald Maitland-Carew inherited the castle in 1972 from his grandmother, the Countess of Lauderdale, he was faced with carrying out repairs on an enormous scale. There were no fewer than forty major outbreaks of dry rot and the central tower was found to be leaning backwards. Captain Maitland-Carew secured substantial grant aid through the Historic Buildings Council, then, in 1984, he gifted the main part of the castle to a charitable trust set up for its preservation. The extent of the work required to restore Thirlestane Castle – which is more like a palace in its grandeur – to its former splendour was truly daunting. After many years of neglect, the vast central tower was in imminent danger of collapse and the building was edging ever closer to becoming a ruin. The repair of the central tower required the insertion of steel support beams and the drilling of the walls to take steel tension cables. The crumbling stonework of the sixteenth-century keep, which had been built of very small stones reused from earlier fortifications, had to be reconstructed also. The restoration work is ongoing, but, unfortunately, another serious outbreak of dry rot has recently closed the castle to visitors.

Castles and Change

> That which is valued by a dominant culture or cultures in society is preserved and cared for; the rest can be mindlessly or purposefully destroyed, or just left to rot.[I]

Historic buildings are symbolic representations of the past; the attitudes towards them that are displayed by governments, society and individuals reflect, to a large extent, their view of history itself. Buildings have a powerful presence in our everyday lives and threats to their continuity are often met with fierce resistance and sadness. However, their significance changes over time. In the aftermath of the Second World War, 'old' usually meant unwanted, whereas now it is more likely to signify cultural heritage. The fact that many of the historic buildings of Scotland were decaying and even being demolished dismayed a few outspoken conservationists, but nothing much was done to save them until the tide of public opinion turned in the 1970s.

The castle literature of Scotland is full of books that illustrate, describe and glorify the iconic buildings that feature on shortbread tins and calendars. But even the most serious of these books, which carefully trace the history of the owners and events of Scottish castles, stops dead at a date that is usually sometime in the nineteenth century, if not much earlier. It is as if time stood still long ago for Scottish castles. Even the eighty-nine-page guidebook for

Barholm Castle before the restoration

Stirling Castle, published by Historic Scotland after their £12 million refurbishment of the castle, omits all mention of this enormous and exciting twenty-first-century project. Yet castles continue to change. They change owners, they change shape, they change function and, in the last fifty years, dozens of castles have changed from a roofless ruin to an inhabited building.

In terms of outcomes, it is a *sine qua non* that things change when a castle is restored. The most noticeable change is usually in the outward appearance of the building; many 'before' and 'after' pictures are radically different, particularly when the building has been harled with lime render for the first time in living memory.

A familiar grey-stone ruin partly covered in ivy and surrounded by long grass and wild flowers may become an imposingly bright-white tower with a formal garden and a car park. Not everyone admires that kind of change. Access to the castle for the local community may change if a ruined castle is restored by individuals for use as a private, family home. Local ruins are often used as playgrounds by adventurous children or as (romantic) trysts by teenagers and adults, and may be sorely missed. On the other hand, local people may be delighted to see that a deteriorating building – maybe even a blot on the landscape – in danger of collapse has been rescued. Inside, the appearance of restored castles is also radically different, perhaps even more so than outside, if the outer grey stone has been left un-rendered. New floors, walls, kitchens and bathrooms are installed, with furnishings brought in to show off the setting.

A few restoring owners made quite radical changes to the structure of their ruined buildings, by removing wings or large sections that had been added at a later date than the original building. Some carried out this demolition work for aesthetic reasons and some for pragmatic ones – to reduce a huge building to a manageable size, say. In fact, many Scottish castles and country houses – if not the majority – have developed organically over the course of several centuries, as architectural taste and the needs of the owners have changed. Who is to say that the stripping back of a building to its 'pure' form is any more authentic than setting it in the aspic of its 'finished' state? Article 11 of the 1964 Venice Charter (to which Britain is a signatory) states that, 'When a building includes the superimposed works of different periods, the revealing of the underlying state can only be justified in exceptional circumstances'. But should a historic building that has been relatively recently added to or changed with unsympathetic materials – dormer windows from the 1960s set in cement-clad surrounds, say – be retained on the grounds that one should not reveal the underlying state? What about a Georgian or Victorian addition that makes the house seem unbalanced – should that be removed?

The owners who removed parts of their castles prior to the restoration – Aboyne, Aiket, Ballencrieff, Cleish, Kinkell, Lochnaw and Methven – all did so for reasons that were carefully considered and which they felt to be entirely justifiable. Some were more successful restorations than others, but all beg the question of where to stop when working with a historic building. There is no easy prescriptive answer, but the question is addressed in a wider, international context by Jukka Jokilehto in *A History of Architectural Conservation*, and in a scholarly and thought-provoking manner by the historian Michael Davis in *The Scottish Castle Restoration Debate 1990–2101*. Davis is admiring of the many successful Scottish castle restorations:

The greatest achievement of the often virtually unknown and largely unobserved phenomenon of Scottish castle restoration in the last five decades has not only been preservation, but a holistic effect, inside and out, which has real claims to art … [T]he results have often been winsome, seductive and highly appealing. (p.70)

Almost all restorers claim to want authenticity in their restored building, although some strive harder than others. 'Authenticity' is one of those multivalent terms that holds a different meaning for each restorer. What most aim for is a return to an idealised original, a recapturing of what is believed once to have been.

Barholm Castle shortly after it was restored

France Smoor, restoring architect of Tilquhillie Castle and Gagie House, warned of 'the romantic preoccupation with one or another period of an historic building [which] often leads the restorer away, trying to peel away subsequent or even previous layers of architecture to achieve an ideal image'.[2] Blackhall Manor, Mains Castle and Ballencrieff Castle were all restored by DIY builders using reclaimed materials that they sourced themselves. At Blackhall Manor, the plumbing, plastering, tile-laying and slating were done by tradesmen; all other work was done by Alex Strachan, the original restoring owner, with volunteer unskilled labour. Around 30,000 bricks and 30 tons of stone, much of it reclaimed, were used. Almost all the timbers, including the beams in the Great Hall, were also reclaimed. At Ballencrieff, little new material was used: old roof slates were purchased, items from other castles bought at auction and flagstones salvaged from churches.

The fact that materials look old, even if they are not necessarily local, or antique, is a significant feature in the judgement of authenticity. The cost of sourcing original Jacobean furniture and artefacts is prohibitive for all but the wealthiest owners, but reproduction pieces often sit well within sixteenth-century walls.

The restoring architects of Garth and Cleish castles, on the other hand, used modern materials and modern design to fill the interior spaces of their late-medieval buildings. Michael Spens, architect and previous owner of Cleish Castle, designed a balcony support in the form of twin steel columns dipped in nickel. The result was a sixteenth-century space augmented by the materials of the present. It received accolades in the international press and won a Saltire Award. This was in the early 1970s; awards for such modernising work would be less likely in the twenty-first century, when faithful reinstatement of the last stage of the building's development is usually required. Cleish had been 'restored' in a bastardised way in the 1840s, with baronial add-ons; Spens stripped away the nineteenth-century additions to create a late twentieth-century interior filled with works of art by the sculptor Eduardo Paolozzi. Although this was not truly a restoration, as Cleish had been continuously occupied before Spens bought it, the changes were as extensive as that involved in many complete restorations of ruinous or derelict buildings. This was a project where contemporary art formed a fundamental part of the structural changes to the building. However, the amazing contemporary Great Hall ceiling that he had commissioned, modelled in shallow relief by Eduardo Paolozzi in 1973, was replaced by a subsequent owner with a traditional painted ceiling in sixteenth-century style by artist Jennifer Merredew. She has completed a number of castle restoration ceilings during the past twenty years, including the one at Barholm Castle. As can be seen from the photograph of Jennifer at work, she does not lie on her back to paint, but rather stands on a sturdy

Interior of Tilquhillie Castle

scaffold, with her neck supported by a surgical collar. Paolozzi's ceiling was later installed in the main hall of the Dean Gallery at The Scottish National Gallery of Modern Art in Edinburgh, where it can be viewed today.

Perhaps the most startling change that has taken place in a Scottish castle is the exterior painting of Kelburn Castle by Brazilian graffiti artists. In 2007, the Earl of Glasgow had been advised that the cement harling (render) of the castle would need to be replaced. His children suggested painting the castle before the harling was removed, and a spectacular spray-painted mural was applied. In 2011, the mural was named as one of the world's top ten examples of street art – on a par with Banksy's

work in Los Angeles. Although it was initially intended to be a temporary covering, the artwork seems set to stay for a while longer, despite rumours that the earl was under pressure to remove it. Historic Scotland's principal inspector for Glasgow and the south west, Ranald MacInnes, said in a letter to *The Scotsman* newspaper:

Historic Scotland has not stepped in and ordered the removal of the graffiti from Kelburn Castle and will not be doing so in the future. We were happy to support this exciting and innovative project. The artwork is a celebration of Kelburn Castle's importance as a historic building and has attracted many visitors to the estate.

One major change that has taken place in Scottish castles since 1945 is the increase in access for the paying public, either as clients in overnight accommodation, wedding guests or day-tripping tourists paying an entry fee to tour the interior. Fifty years ago, perhaps only the queen would have access to more than a handful of Scottish castles for an overnight stay. Now, we can all experience as many nights as we wish in over 150 castles, provided that we are prepared to pay the market rate for the accommodation. Over 150 privately owned castles also currently advertise weddings, which became a particularly attractive proposition for many castles after a change in the law in 2002, allowing marriages to take place in venues other than churches and registry offices. The numbers became

Nineteenth-century engraving of Kelburn Castle

Jennifer Merredew painting the ceiling at Barholm, in 2005

high in a very short period. Clearly, castle weddings are a good commercial prospect. Historic Scotland offers twelve castle venues for weddings, including Edinburgh, Stirling and Urquhart castles. The National Trust for Scotland has eight castles that cater for weddings.

The same view of Kelburn Castle, in 2009

Comlongon Castle is an excellent example of a castle that has capitalised on the wedding market. This large fifteenth-century keep near Annan was abandoned in the sixteenth century. The existing extension was built in 1900. Between 1939 and 1952, it was used by Barnardos as an orphanage and after that, the estate's factor would occasionally live in it, but it had lain empty for ten years after the Earl of Mansfield sold the castle, mansion and estate. The Ptolomy family had previously purchased Knockbrex Castle in Kirkudbrightshire (a nineteenth-century fake castle, locally known as the 'toy fort') and ran it as a small hotel. They were looking for a larger castle when Comlongon came on the market in 1984. Tony Ptolomey and his family refurbished both the castle and the mansion, doing most of the work themselves.

At first, most of the guests in the eleven-bedroomed hotel were American tourists, but, in 1991, Ptolomey was afraid that business would suffer as a result of the recession, and looked around for another source of clientele. 'We advertised in a wedding magazine,' he said, 'and were amazed at the response. We received letters and phone calls from throughout the world. The recession never arrived as far as we were concerned, and our difficulty now is to fit foreign tourists in as well as the weddings.' Three local ministers are needed to handle the number of weddings conducted at Comlongon. Ptolomey says, 'The couples are normally accompanied by close friends and relatives who also stay at the castle, which means that together with tourists we have an occupancy rate of about 90 per cent.'

Restoring owners have opened hotels and upmarket holiday lets and diversified the uses of castles in other ways, including the management of business ventures, such as a deer stud farm (Midmar in Aberdeenshire), a nursery garden (Balbithan) and an architects' practice (Rossend Castle and Liberton House). These examples are of businesses where sales could be enhanced by the siting of the objects for sale beside or within a castle – the grounds or interior of a sixteenth-century tower make a much better venue to view breeding stags, buy garden plants, or visualise a restored building than a fenced farmyard, a purpose-built garden centre or a city office. However, all three have since changed hands and changed their usage, in a nice demonstration of the fluid nature of castle ownership and use in recent times.

The second half of the twentieth century also saw the conservation movement across Britain and Europe start up, gradually swell and finally grow to huge proportions, at the same time as the number of restorations of Scottish castles rose dramatically, decade on decade; the numbers of demolitions dropped equally dramatically. Sales of castles also increased over time – in the 1950s only a handful of castles were sold, rising to over 100 in the 1990s. Was this simply a reflection of the number of general property sales in the period? Or, are these changes cultural as well as economic?

Culturally, much of the story of the heritage movement is shared between Scotland and England. Scotland certainly had its own heritage champions, such as Nigel Tranter and Maurice Lindsay, and its own national and local conservation organisations. However, as a nation it benefited from the broader British campaigning of individuals, including Marcus Binney, Roy Strong and Patrick Cormack, and organisations such as SAVE Britain's Heritage, whose focus was mainly on England, but whose message was disseminated throughout the UK by the media and by those interested in historic buildings who moved between the two countries. The Scottish charitable conservation bodies – the Architectural Heritage Society of Scotland, the Scottish Castles Association, the Scottish Civic Trust, the Scottish Historic Buildings Trust, The Saltire Society and The National Trust for Scotland – all played a role in changing public attitudes and conservation practice, as did a handful of active and influential individuals who campaigned for changes in attitudes towards historic buildings.

In Scotland, unlike England, the sense of national identity is bound up with the iconography of castellated architecture, way beyond the mere romantic attraction of castles. Charles McKean was surprised to find that reaction to *The Scottish Chateau*, published in 2001, differed north and south of the border. Scottish readers focused on the warlike aspect of castles:

It had become clear that these 'castles' were castles only in name, and that, in many cases, such a name was a modern attribution. They were, rather, largely indefensible stately houses or country seats. Yet what extraordinary passion this interpretation provoked ... it was taken as an attack upon the builders of these houses, on their owners, and as an affront to the honour of the country itself. To remove the warlike overcoat of these great houses was tantamount to robbing them of their dignity and personality.[3]

It is not surprising to find that the National Trust for Scotland and Historic Scotland use images of fighting and aggression, all tied up with swords, kilts and tartan bonnets, in their publicity material and in the shops attached to castle ticket offices. Somehow, castles and conflict are inextricably linked in people's minds. Castle owners and their visitors are fascinated by gunloops and the idea of pouring boiling oil over the enemy from the crenellated parapets of their towers, even though such an action may never have occurred to their sixteenth-century counterparts. The insertion of turrets, gunloops and crenellations in many castles was more of an architectural fashion statement than a defensive necessity. However, it seems unlikely that the association between castles and defence will ever be loosened, although academic research shows it to have been much slighter than we would like to think.

By the turn of the twenty-first century, major social, political and economic changes had taken place. The few castle restorations carried out in the 1950s were done in a different social world from those of the 1990s. Standards of living had increased greatly, as had social mobility and educational opportunities. In 1934, *SMT Magazine* was full of praise for the new means of motorised transport as a way of reaching Scotland's historic buildings:

> The facilities which these modern vehicles offer still seem incredible, so perfect are they in design and workmanship and comfort. With the motor coach and car at our disposal, we may now travel in freedom and comfort into the heart of the distant hills, or by the shores of the Western seas, all in a brief day's journey, and still find ample time to visit many of our ancient abbeys and historic castles.[4]

Doubtless, travel by motorcar and charabanc was a thrilling novelty in the 1930s, but it was not until the 1960s that improvements in infrastructure brought about greater ease of transport, through better roads, new bridges, more reliable cars and increased air travel, which, in turn, allowed those with new wealth to buy properties in remote areas and still move around the country efficiently.

The changes of the post-war period are reflected in the challenges and opportunities facing those who restored castles over the decades from the 1950s to the beginning of the twenty-first century. Their restoration stories, decade by decade, are told in later chapters. Mostly, they are tales of triumph, but almost all, like any rattling good yarn, have elements of risk, adventure, conflict and suffering.

The Owners

Who was responsible for these restorations and why? The majority of castle restorers were 'new' owners, with no family connection to the ruined building that they bought and no landowning credentials. There is, of course, no single, simple answer to the question of who they were – the purchasers were as varied as the buildings they bought to restore. In addition, a handful of castles were restored by 'old' owners, whose ancestors had owned the building for generations and a significant minority of restorations, such as Dudhope in Dundee and Pitheavlis in Perth, were carried out by building preservation trusts or local authorities.

The sculptor and artist Gerald Laing, who restored Kinkell Castle in 1969, wrote the first full-length account of restoring a Scottish castle. 'Anyone who rebuilds a castle,' he said, 'is automatically deemed to be either an American, an aristocrat, a businessman, a property speculator, or, at the very least, a Tory.' And, indeed, Laing's castle-rebuilding stereotypes are represented in reality, although not as the whole picture. American restorers and aristocrats together make up a small minority of restorers (three Americans and eight aristocrats). Businessmen – and also businesswomen, but not many of them – and property developers are a much larger group. Some developers were in fact speculators, although the level of both risk and expense involved in restoring a ruined castle means that their numbers were small. Tories are also well represented. Nicholas Fairbairn, who restored Fordell Castle in the early 1960s, was a Tory MP, Peter Clarke of Kirkhope Tower (restored in 1996) had been a Tory candidate, as was Helen Bailey of Borthwick Tower; she was also a businesswoman and an ardent admirer of Margaret Thatcher. Representing another political party,

David Steel, former Liberal leader and first Presiding Officer of the Scottish Parliament, took the title Baron Steel of Aikwood when he was made a life peer in 1997. This was in honour of his home in Aikwood Tower, which he and his wife Judy had restored from a ruin in the 1980s.

Sales of castles, including those restored, rose steadily between 1945 and 2010; like restorations, sales of castles before 1945 were not uncommon, but they were sporadic and usually took place within a closed group of existing landowners, with occasional incursions by the nouveau riche. Earlshall in Fife, for example, was sold to the bleach merchant R.W. McKenzie in 1891, who employed the architect Robert Lorimer to restore it for him. The exuberant painted ceiling in the barrel-vaulted long gallery had decayed almost beyond saving by 1887, when the architects, MacGibbon and Ross,

Ceiling at Earlshall Castle; restored by Robert Lorimer in the nineteenth century

lamented its fragile condition (its loss would have been a tragedy). Lorimer's nineteenth-century restoration, although said to be rather heavy-handed in places, is a triumph.

After 1945, the commercial value of Scottish castles started to appreciate and a much broader cross-section of society began to buy castles. These included the entertainer, Billy Connolly, Harrods owner, Mohammed Al-Fayed, and Body Shop entrepreneur, Anita Roddick, along with many new owners with no particular claim to fame and no previous connections to landed estates or castles. In 2002, the tabloid press reported, in a frenzy of excitement, that Michael Jackson was in a celebrity bidding war with Madonna and golfer, Nick Faldo, over Amhuinnsuidhe Castle, although none of the three purchased it in the end – and perhaps none of them ever intended to. Of all the castles restored between 1945 and 2012, more than fifty were later sold. So, these castles all entered the high-end housing market. Some were sold for sad reasons, such as Fordell, put on the market by Sam Fairbairn

after the death of her husband. A few were restored with the intention of selling on, although mainly the motivations seemed not to be to make money quickly, but rather to make a fine job of restoring a building in need of care. In this category would fall Kit Martin and Nicholas Groves-Raines, both architect serial restorers who bought properties, restored them with great care and sensitivity and sold on to fund the next restoration, although the latter lived in them for some years first. A few were sold because the owner could not afford the upkeep.

The physical difficulties inherent in castle living may even add to their charm when selling, according to estate agent Jamie McNab:

Castle buyers are eccentrics. They're looking at buildings that make very few concessions to modern living ... I sold one castle where the facilities were so primitive that every bedroom needed a potty, which, when they were full, were put in wardrobes to keep the moths away!

Problems and Hardships

Even when the outcome of a castle restoration is a great success, the process of getting there almost certainly involved obstacles to be overcome and problems to be solved, to say nothing of heartache, distress and despair.

John Coyne, restorer of Tilquhillie Castle in Aberdeenshire, claimed:

'Castle restoration is a highly idiosyncratic endeavor, requiring extreme levels of optimism, patience and, above all, tenacity. The obstacles facing prospective restorers are of heroic proportions.' From personal experience and from talking with many castle owners and reading their stories, it is clear that John Coyne has described the difficulties of castle restoration very accurately. The process of restoring a historic building for reoccupation often involves battles, both physical and metaphorical. Physically, many restorers engaged in activities demanding prodigious feats of endurance, singlehandedly hauling huge quantities of rubble around a building site or living in squalid conditions whilst carrying out heavy manual work. Metaphorically, any large building project is apt to present a mountain of difficulties to climb, from financial uncertainties and unforeseen problems to strain on family relationships and exhaustion clouded by pessimism. Administratively, battles with the authorities were a feature of a significant proportion of projects. The individual arguments that simmered or raged between castle owners and the government body, Historic Scotland, play out the larger issues of integrity and continuity, which permeate the debate about how to restore a ruin, and indeed, whether restoration should take place at all.

Gerald Laing's account of the restoration of Kinkell Castle, near Inverness, in the 1960s is full of tales of difficulties faced and obstacles overcome, but he pointed out that his problems were minor compared with those experienced at Kisimul Castle in Barra: 'The castle has a high vaulted Great Hall. A friend of mine visited Macneil and, as they were sitting around the fire talking, he noticed that, not only was the ceiling dripping with moisture, but small clouds were forming high up in the room.'[5]

Hardship, both physical and financial, is a major theme of the individual restorations. Robert Macneil suffered from the effects of clouds during, as well as after, the rebuilding work on Kisimul:

Everything seemed in a conspiracy to make the undertaking difficult. The weather, generally, was very bad. Time after time we had severe gales and driving rains, and there was literally no shelter of any kind in the entire castle, not one spot where we could stand or sit out of the pouring rain or strong winds. All the workmen and I regularly wore heavy oilskins – when we could lay them aside was the exception and not the rule. Despite these trying conditions we went steadily ahead with the work.[6]

The accounts of the restorers almost seem to vie with each other in the extent of their privations and efforts. At Glenapp Castle the work lasted for years, starting in 1994:

The next five and a bit years were a blur of architects, planners, building control inspections, site meetings, consultants, workmen of every description, dirt, mess, power cuts, floods, leaks and all manner of major successes and setbacks. We worked all day and all evening, seven days a week, 365 days a year. Sometimes we weren't off the premises for weeks on end.

Building work at Glenapp Castle in the nineteenth century

At Kinkell:

> Though there was little snow on the ground that year, it was bitterly cold. We made a brazier from an old oil drum and set it in the fireplace of the Great Hall ... During our tea breaks we would huddle round it seated on blocks of wood or stone.[7]

The Stewarts at Ballone also 'roughed it' during the restoration, settling into a tiny self-built bothy next to the castle to begin the massive task of restoration. The bothy had just one big room and they had three small children. In Wales, Judy Corbett and her husband had only just moved in to start camping in their derelict mansion, Gwydir Castle, when disaster struck:

> Jerry came bounding into the room and told us in one, long, sausaged-out sentence, that the river had burst its banks in the night and the garden was completely flooded and that we were cut off from the town and all our garden walls had been washed away and the cellars were full of water and the flood was still rising and some of our furniture was still outside in the courtyard and our car was floating around in the car park. And what did we want him to do? That was the moment reality hit. Not even I could kid myself that there was romance to be found in our current predicament.[8]

In Spain, during the restoration of L'Avenc, Matthew Parris also suffered with the weather, but of a different kind, as he recorded in his diary at the time: 'Only two steps done by lunchtime. Arms ache with lifting. Neck burning. Cicadas screech. Getting hotter ... I'm dirty and sweaty. Contemplate fetching bathing water from cattle trough.'[9]

Financial problems, too, often caused by the scale of the projects, dogged many restorers, although again the scale of them seems almost like a badge of honour rather than a source of terrible complaint:

> Sam recently did a quick count of the rooms, and came up with the astonishing figure of 89. The roof needed immediate attention as it leaked, nearly every room has had to be replastered and redecorated, and wet rot ran riot among the ornate panelling and beams ... 'So far we have spent £150,000 restoring the house, and we've had to sell a couple of our houses to finance it,' she says. 'Everything to do with Duncraig seems to cost a fortune – the wallpaper for the front hall alone cost £3,000.'

In Ireland, Nicholas Browne had also taken on a huge property for restoration, Castle Oliver, and he found himself in difficulties:

You have no fire insurance, no contents insurance, no insurance of any kind, other than for the car. Every penny you raise must go into the building and it is so difficult to pay the regular overheads, like electricity, food, clothing, motoring, etc., etc., that you simply are unable to afford to go on holiday, ever.[10]

Technical problems also doubtless occurred in many projects, but the owners in their narratives tend to see them as challenges with comic potential rather than serious setbacks. Although the stakes were high and the problems seemingly insurmountable in at least some of the projects, most owners appear to have relished the challenges they presented. The castle restorers who struggled and (almost) failed with their difficult rebuilding were emphatic in their defence of the value of what they were doing; the harder things became, the more devoted they were to their projects. In addition to expending gargantuan physical efforts and/or being prey to serious financial problems, many restorers also found themselves in conflict with their neighbours or with the authorities in one way or another.

Battles with the Neighbours

Marigold MacRae, whose husband's grandfather restored Eilean Donan just after the First World War, told the *Scots Magazine* with airy dismissiveness:

'Of course, there were one or two people, back in the 1920s, who grumbled to the newspapers complaining that the MacRaes were spoiling this picturesque old ruin with all their restoration. But all that's forgotten now and I think most people love what's been done.' She is correct in a sense, in that the majority of current visitors to Eilean Donan, perhaps the most iconic of all Scottish castles, simply admire its picturesque form and setting and are probably completely unconcerned about the rebuilding history.

When a ruinous building is rebuilt, the effects ripple out across the wider community. Jeremy Irons hit problems in the local community when he rendered Kilcoe Castle, in Ireland, in a rust colour after reoccupying the building. He had originally decided to keep the bare-stone finish, but was forced to apply the render when it became obvious that water penetration through the walls of his new home could not be prevented otherwise. The naked stone was perceived as being more natural and in keeping with the landscape:

> My neighbour James who has supported my endeavours through thick and thin, doesn't like the colour, but has the good grace to see it as my affair. I hope, though, that he and the many others who have supported so steadfastly my endeavours with the castle and who now feel dismay at the sight of its fruits, will, in time, grow used to Kilcoe's new raiment. Time and the elements will work their unstoppable magic, and just as my mother's new hairdo always looked better the day after it was done, so the castle will look better tomorrow. Change is something I find difficult as the next man and there's no doubt Kilcoe has changed. But it has also renewed itself and, like much of Ireland, become forward-looking and proud of itself.

Jeremy Irons' neighbour may have viewed the colour of Kilcoe's render as a private matter, but in reality, significant changes in large historic buildings in the landscape are of public concern, as they change the environment for all of those in the neighbourhood. After the harling (rendering) of Law Castle in Ayrshire, local feeling was offended:

> A neighbour, who asked not to be named, said Mr. Phillips had wrought havoc. 'He has absolutely ruined what was a lovely old stone castle. It was a work of art, with beautiful stonework that had been there for 500 years, then he came along and roughcast every inch of it.'

Public perceptions of what is an accurate historical representation often differ from what is actually the case, and it is more than likely that Law Castle was originally rendered with harling. When we restored Barholm, a neighbour said, 'It's a pity about the pebble-dashing.' We knew what he meant, but, in fact, the bright tower is now much closer to its original appearance, when it would also have been covered in harling, than when it was as a grey-stone ruin twenty years ago. Similarly, at Stirling Castle – which dominates the landscape for miles – there was initial outrage about the limewash, which was matched to the original colour and applied to the Great Hall when it was restored in 1999. It glows golden in the light and would have signified to all around that this was a spectacular royal building of the highest importance.

While neighbours may be pleased to see a dilapidated building rescued, in some communities there is serious opposition to restoration. Several Scottish restorers – the Jamiesons at Cramond, Peter Hewkin at Craigrownie, the Cowans at Glenapp and the Morrises at Balgonie – were the target of local vandals, suffering mindless damage to their property. Being a castle owner runs the risk of inciting aggression from neighbours, or the 'politics of envy' as Nicholas Fairbairn claimed about his purchase and restoration of Fordell Castle.

Helen Bailey suffered the trauma of having her water supply at Borthwick Castle deliberately cut, as did Matthew Parris in Spain, who finally instituted a prolonged and ultimately unsuccessful legal battle to regain it. In the village of Portencross in Ayrshire, residents formed the campaign group, Friends of Portencross (FOPC), when the ruined Portencross Castle was put up for sale in 1998. They fought a vigorous and finally successful campaign against the sale of the castle to an individual buyer from Canada, who had plans and the financial wherewithal to restore the building as a family home, and were forthright in the expression of their fears:

> Last weekend, I met an 84-year-old lady sitting on a chair in the car park just enjoying the scenery because she had been coming to this spot since she was a little girl ... Our concern is that all that will end if it is bought as private property by some individual whose ego demands he puts up fences to keep the public out ... Others, feared Mr Proven, might want to make it into a holiday home 'and play lord of the manor, coming across from time to time to see how the serfs are getting on'.

In 2007, when it seemed that Dumfries House and its contents might be sold off at auction to private individuals, an entry on the website of the *Scotsman* newspaper 'Drive to save Dumfries House for Nation' comments section read: 'If it's a National Treasure, it's OORS!!! Hands off!!' Dumfries House did finally become 'oors', due to the timely intervention of Prince Charles.

Life in a Sixteenth-Century Castle

The problems of living today in a late-medieval tower include: battles with damp penetration through thick, stone walls that have been rain-soaked for centuries, ineffective (or horribly costly) heating systems and general inconvenience. But these pale into insignificance compared with life at the time it was built. One feature that all twenty-first-century restored castles have in common is modern amenities. All have kitchens with fridges, and cookers that work, more or less, efficiently. They have bathrooms with baths and showers served with hot and cold running water, flushing toilets, electric lighting, heating that is usually powered by a central boiler, and most have comfortable armchairs from which to watch television or work on computers. In order to get to and from their castle, owners drive along paved roads in their cars, parking close to the door in order to offload the latest supermarket weekly shop.

Contrast all of these comforts, which we take for granted, with daily life in the sixteenth century. While life would have been immeasurably more comfortable for the inhabitants of castles and towers than for the neighbouring peasants in their windowless mud and thatch hovels, conditions would nonetheless have been very difficult by today's standards. One major difference would have been the lack of light. Glass was very expensive and only available in small panes. Most sixteenth-century

Even a new-build tower, Craigietocher, has had half-shuttered windows installed for authenticity (Courtesy of Michael Davis)

The Great Hall fire at Barholm

houses had wooden shutters with no glazing at the bottom part of the window and a few panes of crude glass or translucent animal hide or horn above. At Barholm we installed this type of window in the Great Hall, as there was evidence that this had been the type used originally, although of course we were allowed to fill the leaded frames with modern glass. All the same, the unglazed part lets in draughts and no light at all. Similar windows can be seen in properties owned by the National Trust, such as Gladstone's Land in Edinburgh's Royal Mile and the Palace of Culross in Fife.

Light in the castle would have been provided by tallow candles and oil lamps, both of which would smell of animal fat, probably rancid. On special occasions, when we light dozens of candles and turn off the electric lights, the interior of Barholm may look romantic and special, but it is also very difficult to see, and could quickly become depressing without any prospect of better illumination. Similarly with heating. The Great Hall fire looks wonderful blazing with logs and there is nothing nicer than to sit in front of it on a cold winter's evening. But once the logs burn away – which they do remarkably quickly – if they are not replaced it quickly becomes cold, and if the underfloor heating is not working, the temperature even a few feet away from the hearth drops dramatically. There is clear evidence that all of the fireplaces of Barholm Castle had been significantly reduced in size at some time, presumably to save fuel. The stair tower is always cold, as it is almost impossible to heat. Fires were dangerous, too. The commonest cause of death for a medieval woman (after childbirth) was her heavy skirts and petticoats going up in flames as she tended the cooking pot over an open fire. At Barholm, we are not allowed to have open fires in the bedrooms, because of contemporary building regulations (the stone hearths are not big enough); we also had to apply for 'relaxations' to allow us to retain smaller windows than are normally allowed and lack of statutory fire exits.

However draughty and dark the interior of the sixteenth-century tower house was, the interior decoration would have been bright and welcoming. Walls were plastered and painted or lined with wood panelling (not bare rubble, as popular imagination has it) and covered with such tapestries and paintings as the owners could afford, with ceilings and wall panels often colourfully painted. The lairds of the larger houses, at least, were cultured people, who travelled widely and drew inspiration from European design. We know from contemporary inventories that they valued silver, pewter, fine linens, luxurious embroidered textiles and richly carved furniture. Life may not have been as comfortable as we know it today, but in a sixteenth-century castle owned by a person of rank, life would have been as comfortable as they could make it.

CHAPTER 2

THE BUILDINGS

Scottish Castles and Tower Houses

The most significant feature of Scottish castles, in terms of their manageability as private restorations, is the domestic scale of so many of them – some are quite tiny – especially compared to the huge

Rusco Tower
in Galloway

size of most European castles. This has doubtless been a major contributory factor in the post-Second World War 'renaissance' of Scottish castles. The majority of castles that were reoccupied from ruins are small or medium sixteenth-century tower houses. Most had not been centres of power, but rather peripheral parts of great estates (e.g. Aikwood or Kirkhope in the Borders, both part of the Buccleuch estates), or had been abandoned by the families for more modern, grander and more convenient houses in the eighteenth and nineteenth centuries (e.g. Barholm or Tilquhillie in Aberdeenshire).

During the sixteenth century, the peak of the building boom occurred after the death of Mary, Queen of Scots, in the Jacobean period after 1570. Tower building carried on through the first quarter of the seventeenth century, but by the mid-seventeenth century, the tower had generally become unfashionable as a domestic residence and lower, more convenient country houses were being designed. Scottish castles varied in size and style, from the tiny to the massive, and from the starkly plain to the ornate Renaissance palace, but the sixteenth-century Scottish tower house has an instantly recognisable form. Indeed, at first blush one might look much the same as the next, although on closer inspection the surprising thing is the multitude of differences in detail and style among them.

Although most tower houses stand tall and imposing, dominating the surrounding landscape in splendid isolation, their modern appearance belies the context in which they developed. Firstly, many tower houses, Barholm included, probably started out as square, squat fifteenth-century buildings with a wooden external stair, such as Liberton Tower in Edinburgh, restored in the 1990s.

Later, in the sixteenth century, they would have had additional storeys, stair towers and cap houses added, to reflect demands for increased comfort, space and style, while a diminishing threat of war or attack meant that military symbols, such as crenellations and gunloops, could be ornamental rather than real. What all tower houses had 500 years ago, and very few still have today, is a range of enclosures and outbuildings, which housed the kitchen, dairy, bakehouse, alehouse, doocot (dovecot), kennels,

Gilknockie Tower in the Borders, also known as Hollows Tower

stables, servants' quarters and other necessary offices that could not be accommodated within the walls of the tower. Within the shelter of the high enclosure walls were a series of yards, including gardens, where – in the wealthier properties at any rate – artichokes, peaches, asparagus and other exotic delicacies were grown, as well as the more everyday herbs, fruit and vegetables.

Visiting a tower for the first time is always an adventure, full of puzzles, surprises and riddles. One of the biggest mysteries at our tower, Barholm, is why we have a garderobe waste chute that can only have come from the wall walk at the top of the tower – which itself is only accessible by climbing out of a window in the roof. A more inconvenient place for

Tower of Hallbar in Renfrewshire

Dean Castle in Ayrshire

a toilet is hard to imagine, especially when the other chute connects to a nice sit-down loo with a moss-box recess carefully set into the stone beside it (moss being a medieval substitute for soft toilet paper). We also have a wonderfully ornate front door with a mysterious creature and two faces carved into it, joined by rope moulding. For a small laird's tower this is just too elaborate and must surely have come from somewhere else – a dissolved monastery perhaps – rather than being specially commissioned for Barholm. Every tower and castle has its own set of architectural improbabilities about which researchers and the owners can only speculate.

A recent trip to Garlies Castle, a ruin in the wilds of Galloway, provoked much puzzlement among a group of us from the Scottish Castles Association. There, firmly set in the south wall on the ground floor, was a very fine Renaissance fireplace, which was absolutely in keeping with other clear signs of sixteenth-century construction and with lots of evidence that this had once been a grand house. Except that it was in the wrong place – the roof timber supports and the remains of an internal wall meant that the fireplace was at the back of a narrow corridor, when it should have been in the middle of a wall on the floor above, at great-hall level.

Why would such a beautiful and significant feature have been put there? Could subsequent changes to the building somehow have consigned it to its current position? Again, the physical evidence made that seem unlikely. As soon as we got home, we did what we should have done before setting out and read up about Garlies in the reference books. The mystery was soon solved: according to a nineteenth-century account, the fireplace had been moved there 'for preservation' after it was uncovered during archaeological excavations. The lesson here is that one should never make assumptions about a building without checking every available piece of written evidence.

Many of the restored small towers are tiny, with scarcely more accommodation than a modern two- or three-bedroom house. Barns Tower, restored by the Landmark Trust, has only one bedroom (which includes the bathtub inside it), plus a sitting room and a kitchen/dining room. The Tower of Hallbar, restored by the Vivat Trust, looks imposing, but sleeps only five, and sleeping in the top bedroom involves a walk in the open across the parapet to the nearest bathroom. Not many towers are quite so diminutive, but with only one room, or at most two, on each floor in most buildings, space is tight, and the thicker the walls the less space inside. Liberton Tower and Niddry Castle are both imposing fourteenth-century buildings with extremely thick walls; their internal accommodation is remarkably domestic in scale, given the external appearance, like a grapefruit with lots of pith and surprisingly little fruit. At Barholm, which looks very large from the outside, the ground-floor kitchen area is only

The door at Barholm Castle

Wonderfully carved Renaissance fireplace at Garlies Castle, in a mysterious position

one third of the footprint of the building – two thirds is wall.

Some of the larger buildings present a great challenge to the restorer because of the multiplicity of stages of construction (e.g. Ravenstone in Wigtownshire), or the vast scale of the internal accommodation, such as Duncraig Castle in the Highlands and Taymouth Castle in Perth and Kinross, which for several years has been the subject of planned restoration schemes for a luxury hotel that has not yet materialised. The last two are Victorian baronial mansions – castles that never had any need for fortification. There is a snobbery about such buildings, which have been scorned by arbiters of 'good taste' and Modernists, at least until recently.

In the decades following the Second World War, Scots Baronial reached its nadir of esteem, being seen as mad, bad or simply tasteless. At that time it was often considered a mark of good taste to have demolished a house by David Bryce, the arch-Scots baronialist of the High Victorian period. To many Modernists, Scots baronial seemed to embody the most extreme excesses of Victorian architecture. To others, it seemed immoral, irrelevantly linked to an obsolete class, architecturally nationalist rather than international, and apparently contributing nothing to the evolution of modernity.[II]

Fortunately, Bryce and Burn houses are beginning to have a revival of fashion, and houses such as Strathendry Castle and Glenapp are cared for and valued now, rather than a cause for embarrassment for their owners.

Across the country, Scotland's castles are clustered in certain geographic areas. The three main areas where castles have been restored are Aberdeenshire, Dumfries and Galloway, and Edinburgh and the Lothians. The geographical spread of the restored castles is roughly reflected in the spread of all castles throughout Scotland, however, so it seems that there are no areas specially favoured by restorers.

It is, of course, those buildings with 'scenic value' that are most attractive as potential homes to those with the desire to rebuild. Most buildings that have already been restored are attractive and well situated, such as Abbot's Tower in Dumfriesshire, near the romantic ruins of Sweetheart Abbey, or Ackergill Tower in Wick, situated on the Caithness coast. There is a trade-off between costs and scenic location; the more attractive the rural or seaside location and the larger the amount of land included, the higher the value of the building. A few castles, such as Newmilns Tower in Ayrshire, are situated on small plots of land in the centre of busy towns or

Ravenstone
Castle

Strathendry Castle, with additions
by Burn & Bryce

housing estates or within industrial complexes. Many towers and castles have modern farm buildings right up close (these include Barholm, Abbot's Tower, Tillycairn and Terpersie) and this can cause problems of access and lack of space for the building to be properly situated in its rural setting. Some buyers pay relatively low prices for buildings in crowded or unattractive areas – for example, Niddry Castle near Edinburgh, which is next to a shale bing, stark in the landscape at first, but now beginning to mellow. Several castles that remain as potentially restorable ruins tend to have intractable problems of location, for instance Baltersan, which is close to the busy A77 trunk road and has only a tiny footprint of land with no access road, Dunskey, which is situated on a dramatic clifftop, near Portpatrick overlooking the Irish Sea has no easy access for services, and Dunglass lies in the remains of an oil terminal.

The Castle in Fiction

Several mid-twentieth-century novels were structured around the theme of the difficulty landed families had in hanging on to houses that had become too costly to maintain in the twentieth century. Evelyn Waugh's novel, *Brideshead Revisited*, written in 1944, captured aristocratic decline in the story of Brideshead, an English stately home owned by the Flyte family. Only Rex Mottram, the wealthy Canadian outsider, understood that the Flytes were heading for financial collapse:

> Everyone of that sort is poorer than they were in 1914, and the Flytes don't seem to realize it ... Look at the way they live – Brideshead and Marchmain House both going full blast, pack of foxhounds, no rents raised, nobody sacked, dozens of old servants doing damn all, being waited on by other servants.[12]

In 1981, the nation was thrilled by the television adaptation of *Brideshead Revisited*, which played a significant role in glamorising historic houses and arousing interest in the maintenance of heritage.

Waugh's fictional account is echoed by the reality of the Duke of Bedford's grandfather, who was still living at Woburn all alone, with fifty indoor servants and more than 200 outdoor servants, in 1939. Ten rooms were taken up by the six nurses who watched over him in three shifts. When he died, death duties meant that Woburn could only be retained by the family if it became a money-making proposition; a theme that runs through any study of change in the status and ownership of both English and Scottish castles and great houses since the Second World War. It has been claimed that inheritance tax ruined more castles than Oliver Cromwell. Certainly, taxation has caused more changes than many other factors, but it is not the whole story of how and why so many Scottish castles declined (more than fifty were demolished after 1950 and more than fifty are still at risk of collapse) and why so many others were rescued from the brink of ruin.

In 1949, Dodie Smith's novel *I Capture the Castle* was published to critical acclaim. The novel went on to become an immediate bestseller and was nominated in *The Sunday Times* Christmas Books of the Year feature, boosting sales even further for 1950. The story of a family trapped by poverty in a semi-derelict castle and saved by wealthy Americans became a classic romance that has never been out of print; it was first staged as a Broadway play in 1952 and made into a successful movie in 2003. In the same year, the novel was voted by the British public as one of the nation's 100 best-loved novels as part of the BBC's The Big Read. Both the quality of Dodie Smith's writing and the pacy narrative are, of course, critical features in the enduring popularity of the story; but the setting of the romantic, decaying castle captivated readers and touched a nerve in the public consciousness.

In 1952, Alan Melville's play, *Castle in the Air*, about an aristocratic owner trying to sell his dilapidated castle to a wealthy American woman was released as a popular light comedy film starring Margaret Rutherford and David Tomlinson, and the following year, P.G. Wodehouse's novel *Ring for Jeeves*, with a remarkably similar plot, was published. In *Ring for Jeeves* the central theme is the Earl of Rowcaster's financial problems with Rowcaster Abbey. ('Its architecture was thirteenth-century, fifteenth-century and Tudor, its dilapidation twentieth-century post-World War Two.') Getting rid of the building rather than saving it was his primary aim; the happy ending involves a wealthy American widow transporting the building to the United States to rebuild it there. Perhaps it was influenced by *The Ghost Goes West*, a 1936 movie directed by René Clair, in which a poor Scotsman sells the family castle to a rich American millionaire, who has the castle moved to the United States stone by stone. (The difficulty is that the castle is haunted, and the ghost moves with the castle to its new locale.)

Americans to the rescue was clearly a theme with a popular appeal. Only three of the post-war castle restorers have been Americans, however – Dr John Coyne of Tilquhillie, Ann Tweedy Savage of Harthill and Harry Boswell of Balmuto – and only a handful of Americans have bought 'trophy castles', despite occasional scaremongering in the media about Scottish heritage being snapped up by the USA.

Such is the degree to which the castle restorer has become an almost iconic character in modern times that one has become a fictional hero – or perhaps anti-hero would be more accurate. Jane Stevenson's character, David

Laurence, is a conservation architect and the narrator of her witty comic novella 'Light My Fire'. He bought the dilapidated Kilmollich Tower in the north-east of Scotland from a pair of elderly farmers with the intention of transforming it as cheaply and quickly as possible. Throughout, Stevenson provides rich details of the interior and its transformation: 'The kitchen was ghastly, even by the standards of the house as a whole. The walls were covered in pine-panel-effect vinyl paper, and the floor with brown and white tile-effect vinyl. It was a melancholy thought that it was probably laid over good slate slabs.'

Laurence, the architect with a keen sense of social status and style, is a cheat in every sense of the word and gets his comeuppance in the denouement, when disaster strikes just as he is showing a potential purchaser around. A couple of years later, American author Tina Rosenberg was inspired by a visit to Glenapp Castle Hotel to write a novel set in the castle, *Glenapp Castle: A Scottish Intrigue*, featuring the thinly disguised tale of its real-life restorers as background to her ghost story; in this novel, however, the owner-restorers are given deferential treatment and presented as heroic. Both accounts – fictional and autobiographical – of the first view of Glenapp by the would-be restorers emphasise its fairy-tale, romantic qualities: '... the castle floated on air like a mirage with no beginning and no end, melding with the cloudless lapis sky in a blurred, edgeless watercolour. With twin turrets poised like regal bookends, Glenapp Castle seemed the most beautifully proportioned house I had ever seen.'[13]

The History of Castle Restoration

Castle restoration is not a new phenomenon. However, 'adaptation' is a better term for most of the building work carried out in the seventeenth, eighteenth and nineteenth centuries; late medieval stone towers tend to be inconvenient buildings for family living and castle owners have always altered and added to their buildings, as social needs and architectural fashions have changed. In the 1780s, George Paterson was unusual in his restoration of fifteenth-century Castle Huntly, near Dundee (now used as a prison), at a time when Adam mansions were consigning many towers to unfashionable oblivion. However, tradition still had a strong hold in Scotland, particularly when combined with ancient lineage. Charles Wemyss proposed that the ancient Scottish nobility, like the French *noblesse d'épée*, retained the old styles of building as symbolic of their lineage, while the newly wealthy and ennobled (the *noblesse de robes* in France) were building new country houses in the classical style.

It was not until 1843 that the first 'pure' restoration of a roofless tower, without additions or alterations, was carried out, at Cleish Castle. This was followed by the significant rebuilding of ruinous Kilberry Castle (which was essentially a newbuild) and by a trickle of other antiquarian restorations (Castle Stewart in 1869; Old Place of Mochrum in 1873; Barnbougle in 1881), all done for wealthy landowners to enhance their estates – Barnbougle was restored to create a secluded library annexe, for example. Throughout the nineteenth century, forty-five castles were restored, the majority after 1850, although 'restoration' often meant changing the building from its original conception quite radically and adding wings and extra accommodation. In the first half of the twentieth century, thirty were restored, compared to more than four times that figure in the second half of the century.

In 1887–92, architects David MacGibbon and Thomas Ross published the beautifully illustrated five volumes of *The Castellated and Domestic Architecture of Scotland from the Twelfth*

Portencross Castle being restored, 2010

to the Eighteenth Century. Their aim was not simply to provide a detailed description of the state of Scotland's castles, however; this was a plea based on dismay, a precursor of the late twentieth-century heritage campaigns:

It is greatly to be regretted that most of our ancient edifices are rapidly passing away, either from natural decay or other destructive causes. Even since our sketches were made, many have disappeared either in whole or in part ... We are not without hope that this work may serve to direct the attention of proprietors and others to the value of our ancient domestic remains, and may thus help to preserve some of them from the decay and demolition which at present threaten speedily to overtake the greater number. Such a result would be most gratifying, not only to us, but to everyone interested in our national history.[14]

Were they right to be concerned and were their hopes realised – did proprietors consequently take action to save their castles? In the late 1970s, 1980s and 1990s, MacGibbon and Ross were credited with fostering interest in castle restoration, along with Nigel Tranter's five volumes on *The Fortified House in Scotland*, and may thus have been at least indirectly responsible for several projects. But how much impact did they have in the last quarter of the nineteenth century? It can be

argued that the publication of their five-volume magnum opus was one pivotal point in the history of building conservation in Scotland. On a simple count of castles restored from a ruinous state between 1800 and 1945, the majority of rebuilding was carried out between 1887 and 1920, i.e. the thirty years or so after publication. During these years, twenty-nine castles were rescued from ruin or dereliction and restored in some way or another – an average of one per year. However, although MacGibbon and Ross were running a busy architectural practice, they failed to capitalise on the prestigious country house/castle restoration market themselves (apart from Crosbie Castle), despite the fact that they did receive many promising commissions. David Walker, in his detailed history of MacGibbon and Ross' architectural practice, cannot account for this failure: 'Their fame as authors brought in a flood of commissions, some of the greatest promise, which for one reason or another either did not go ahead or were handed on to others to finish.'[15]

MacGibbon and Ross' younger contemporary, Robert Lorimer, seized the opportunities to work on castles and country houses. It is likely that he received commissions because of his skilful social networking; he was friendly, for example, with the wealthy Glasgow shipowner and philanthropist, William Burrell, who endowed the Glasgow Burrell Collection. But a lack of tact lost him the commission for the large refurbishment of Burrell's

Hutton Castle in the Borders, between 1916 and 1930. His chief draughtsman recalled that Lorimer could be 'terrible with clients: in the course of a disagreement on the design he said to one "This house will be remembered because I designed it, not because you paid for it" – he actually said that'.[16]

Perhaps MacGibbon and Ross displayed even more maladroitness towards clients, in order to fare worse than Lorimer. Success in architectural practice is as much about social and political skills and clever project management as design talent – only the very best architects successfully combine both. Lorimer, a great admirer of William Morris, worked on sixteen Scottish castles and was certainly the most productive architect of his time in the field of conservation architecture. From the age of 14, family holidays were spent restoring Kellie Castle in Fife, on which his father had taken a lease. This was something that would strongly influence his early architectural work. Walker claims that Lorimer's restorations were authentic, and so they were in relation to other architects, but McKean sees it differently: 'However picturesque their "restorations" might have been, and however faithful to the Arts and Crafts philosophy of "truth to materials" (another death knell for harling), they were fundamentally unscholarly. They "restored" what they saw solely on the basis of intuition and sensibility'.[17] The same criticism might well be applied to many twentieth-century restorations; rebuilding in a manner that is both scholarly and true is a gold standard that is a rarity, if not an impossibility.

Robert Lorimer was the most prolific architect working on restorations, but many others contributed to the rebuilding of castles for various grandees. Matthews and MacKenzie restored Inglismaldie for the Earl of Kintore in 1882; the firm of Ross and MacBeath restored both Kilcoy and Kinlochaline in 1890 and Sir John Burnet took on Duart for Sir Fitzroy MacLean. Eilean Donan was restored from 1912–32 by George Mackie Watson for Colonel MacRae Gilstrap. Do-it-yourself projects by relatively cash-strapped new owners had not yet begun, but in the heyday of twentieth-century restorations in the 1970s, '80s and '90s, a significant minority of 'new owner' projects were carried out without using a firm of architects as project managers, although most had a friendly architect from whom they bought plans and occasional advice. On the other hand, several of the castles restored after the Second World War were bought by architects, who possessed, presumably, the knowledge and professional expertise to organise the work independently.

MacGibbon and Ross had suggested that the reason for the neglect of Scotland's castellated buildings 'probably arises, to some extent, from their bearing on the architectural and natural history of Scotland not being sufficiently understood and appreciated'.[18] In 1939, Scott-Moncrieff proposed a more robustly expressed explanation: 'all over the Lowlands the survivors of such houses [i.e. towers and mansions] are still left to fall into ruin: an awful reflection of our aesthetic sluggardliness.'[19] Lack of understanding and 'aesthetic sluggardliness' – a wonderfully acerbic term – boil down to much the same thing as explanations: ignorance, which may be claimed as a justifiable excuse and a cause for future optimism, if only education – or a social revolution, such as William Morris hoped for – would prevail.

A nineteenth-century attempt to sell Broughty Castle, a coastal fortress near Dundee, as a restoration project failed: 'By 1821 it was a roofless ruin and was offered for sale in the *Dundee, Perth and Coupar Advertiser* on 21 December as a potentially "delightful residence" capable of restoration at small expense, or "which would make an excellent situation for an inn". There were no takers.'[20] This is a nice illustration of changes in attitudes towards ruined castles. If it had been for sale at any time in the late twentieth century, there would almost certainly have been intense interest and competition to buy and restore it, from a variety of people with no landowning connections. A local community group might also be formed to try to save it, as was the case with Portencross Castle, a somewhat similarly situated building, in 1998.

Broughty Castle was bought by the War Office in 1855, at a time of renewed threat from the French and was surrounded with batteries of large naval guns. It remained in military use until 1949. In 1969 Broughty Castle opened to the public as a museum operated by Dundee Council.

Broughty Castle in Dundee

In Germany in the nineteenth century, Prussian nobles were establishing a castles cult as part of a conservative political movement, suffused with romanticism, aristocratic ambition and a romantic yearning for an ideal age. Robert Taylor described 'monument fever' when nobles began to acquire ruins along the banks of the Rhine to restore. He ascribed the movement to a reaction to growing challenges to the status of the nobility in the nineteenth century: 'Restoring or building castles or just preserving their ruins was one way in which they tried to legitimize their social and political *raison d'être*. They hoped that their rebuilt castle would be an effective "symbol of power".[21]

This was not so long before the time when MacGibbon and Ross were lamenting the sorry state of Scotland's castles; despite the numbers of restorations increasing from 1870–1914 there was only a handful in each decade and nothing that could be called a movement, although Ranald MacInnes identified the years after 1911 in Scotland as 'the climax of another grandiose fashion, namely the "restoration" of fantasy castles in rock-faced rubble'.[22] In the castle restorations of the second half of the twentieth century in Scotland, some of the inspirational factors that Taylor ascribed to the Prussian 'cult' chime well with the Scottish situation (a romantic yearning for an ideal age, bourgeois pretension, nationalistic pride and scholarly interest, in particular), but the root cause, of aristocratic status legitimisation, was very different.

In Ireland, a romantic yearning for an ideal age, bourgeois pretension, nationalistic pride and scholarly interest also describe very well the motives for William Butler Yeats' restoration of his tower, Thoor Ballylee, in the same period as the Prussian nobles were asserting their status through castle restoration. In Romania, Queen Marie, granddaughter of Queen Victoria, restored Castle Bran, which had been gifted to her in 1920 by the City of Brasov. It had been one of the seven strongholds built by the Knights of the Teutonic Order and had never been lived in, although its foundations dated back to the Crusades. It is also known as 'Castle Dracula' as it was once the home of Vlad the Impaler. Queen Marie wrote about the experience in her memoirs:

Queen Marie, Nicholas and Ileana
(Library of Congress, LC-DIG-ggbain-29805)

Oh! with what joy and interest I set about making my Bran livable, putting in certain comforts, letting in more light, repairing the shaky galleries, creating new rooms in odd corners; making use of the huge timbered loft, using waste spaces, digging out secret little passages and stairs, turning queer little dungeons into living-rooms, but withal taking greatest care to preserve the austere, primitive aspect of the place. We have a dear old architect belonging to our house-hold, inherited from King Carol's times. He, too, had always dreamed that one day it would be granted him to repair an old castle; now this quaint building has become his pet work. He has settled down there like an owl in an old wall and devotes all his love, all his skill, to make a real treasure out of my precious little place. But we are in no hurry to complete our work, we are like children with a beloved toy of which we never weary; each year we improve something, without allowing its original aspect to change. It is still the impregnable, pugnacious little fortress, but now it has been given a soul, its eyes are open, it is wide awake, joyfully alive.[23]

In Queen Marie's account, although marked by differences of time, distance, resources and culture, can be seen the same threads of romance, anti-modernism, adventure and fun that are present in so many of the recent Scottish stories. The metaphor of the castle as a toy, as a pet, then as a person is echoed in some of the personifications in later narratives – for example, Judy Corbett likened Gwydir Castle to a small child, Robert Lister Macneil planned to 'wake Kisimul from a long sleep' and Nicholas Fairbairn described Fordell Castle as a 'great and glorious stone womb'.

The Romance of Ruins

In a visual world, we are assailed by images of the castle, in art, the Internet, movies and throughout the media.

The wonderfully atmospheric early nineteenth-century painting, *The Bard* by John Martin, depicting wild romance, is readily recognisable as an image that conjures up the essence of 'castle'. Distant and inaccessible, it nonetheless draws the viewer right into the scene, where it towers above the landscape. Martin's castle might be the model for Hogwarts, the sinister and dangerous castle in the Harry Potter films. Movies present a fantasy version of life and those that feature castles tend to be especially heavy on fantasy. However, there is an alternative view of the castle, in England at least. Sir Nikolaus Pevsner, arch arbiter of historical architectural taste in the mid-twentieth century, described

Haddon Hall as 'the English castle par excellence, not the forbidding fortress on an unassailable crag, but the large, rambling, safe, grey, lovable house of knights and their ladies'.[24] The key word here is 'English'; it is difficult to think of a Scottish castle that might be described in such terms, although Culzean Castle might just make it, despite its unassailable crag; the Robert Adam architecture, disguising a medieval tower house, and the lush terraced gardens make it seem 'safe'.

Broadly speaking, Scottish castles come in three main forms: the medieval fortress, such as Edinburgh Castle; the turreted tower, such as Amisfield; or the Balmorial mansion. None is 'safe, grey and lovable' in the way of a Jacobean English manor.

The romantic view of ruins seen in picturesque eighteenth- and nineteenth-century art was also reflected in poetry, as in this verse of 1766 by John Cunningham:

Elegy on a Pile of Ruins
In the full prospect yonder
  hill commands,
O'er barren heath and
  cultivated plains,
The vestige of an ancient
  abbey stands,
Close by a ruin'd castle's
  rude remains

Ruined castles exert a special fascination. During the Romantic movement and the pursuit of the picturesque in the second half of the eighteenth century, ruins of all kinds became the objects of

Culzean Castle

The Magdaleneklause in Munich, designed and built as a ruin in 1725.

poetry and art and literature in Britain and throughout Western Europe; this heightened awareness of the morbid beauty to be found in decaying architecture carried on through the nineteenth and twentieth centuries. Christopher Woodward, in his all-embracing book on ruins, traced the history of pleasure in ruins from *The Duchess of Malfi* (1617) through Horace Walpole, the Wordsworths, Edgar Allen Poe, William James and others, including Charles Dickens, who extolled the beauty of the Coliseum in his *Letters from Italy* (1846):

> It is the most impressive, the most stately, the most solemn, grand, majestic, mournful sight, conceivable. Never, in its bloodiest prime,

can the sight of the gigantic Coliseum, full and running over with the lustiest life, have moved one heart, as it must move all who look upon it now, a ruin. GOD be thanked: a ruin![25]

Landowners in the eighteenth and nineteenth centuries built fake ruins on their estates; even in the twenty-first century, a company called Redwood Stone manufactures garden ruins and advertises them in glossy magazines. In 2010, the queen officially opened The Queen's Garden in Enfield, London, intended as a visitor attraction for the London Olympics, with its backdrop of a fake, ruined, fourteenth-century manor house built on a lavish scale by Redwood Stone.

The attraction of the manufactured ruin is longstanding; nearly 300 years before, in 1725, the Magdalenenklause in Munich was built for the Elector Max Emanuel in the grounds of Schloss Nymphenburg; it is one of the earliest examples in Europe of a park building consciously designed as a ruin. The hermitage-style building, with its grotto chapel, was intended as a place for the religious contemplation of the transitory nature of earthly lives.

In the twentieth century, Rose Macaulay's sumptuously illustrated book, *Pleasure of Ruins*, which spanned the world in search of photogenic ruins, was partly the result of a personal Christian reawakening, in which she emphasised the spiritual aspects of ruins as well as the aesthetic. Her book was first published in 1953, and republished in 1964 and 1977 in Britain and the USA; it was also published in Dutch and French. Clearly, the subject of ruins had a wide appeal. Many of the Scottish castle restorers specifically mention the romantic aspect of the ruin, which they bought for restoration. Sadly, unless action is taken to stabilise and support many of Scotland's ruins in private ownership, they will inevitably deteriorate and eventually crumble.

The Tower in History

The tower has a long history in popular culture, and a special place in the castellology of Scotland, where towers, both ruinous and occupied, feature prominently in the rural landscape. In an extended essay that bridges literary theory, history and psychology, Theodore Ziolkowski described the towers belonging to four great creative minds of the early twentieth century (the poets W.B. Yeats, Robinson Jeffers and Rainer Maria Rilke, and the psychoanalyst, Carl Jung) and presented a seductive series of arguments portraying the significance of the tower as an anti-modernist image. He traced the history of the tower from the earliest times: in the sixteenth century, the tower was a common subject in European art, particularly the Biblical Tower of Babel. The tower became a symbol of religious renewal for Protestantism, through Martin Luther.

In his tower in Wittenberg, in 1513, he underwent what German theologians call his Turmerlebnis ('tower experience') – the insight that the true path to salvation leads through faith. The history of art and literature is richly populated with towers, symbolising power, sexuality, refuge and spirituality at various times in different genres.

William Beckford's gigantic tower of 1801 at Fonthill Abbey, in Wiltshire[26], erected as a private temple to the arts in Gothic Revival style (not an abbey in the religious sense), is a symbolic example of the desire of a very rich man to build very, very high. He had 500 labourers working in day and night shifts. The tower reached 90m before it collapsed. The front door was 10m high – the height of four storeys of our tower at Barholm. Six years later a new tower, also 90m high, was

Fonthill Abbey (Delineations of Fonthill and its Abbey)

built and it too collapsed. The third tower took seven years to build and finally collapsed in 1825 – but only after Beckford had sold the building to a munitions dealer, due to the loss of two of his sugar plantations. Sadly, there is virtually nothing left of Fonthill Abbey today.

The Restored Buildings

The great majority of castles restored and reoccupied after 1945 are small- and medium-sized sixteenth-century towers – none on the extreme scale of Fonthill. Only three buildings date exclusively from the nineteenth century, Duncraig, Glenapp and Craigrownie, which is probably more to do with availability, costs and practicalities rather than aesthetics, however. Derelict Victorian mansions are usually too big to be conveniently used as a modern family home; the scale of work needed, if dry and/or wet rot is established, in a huge building is beyond the capacity of most individuals. The rather tragic story of the Dobsons of Duncraig, a family who took on a vast, decaying castellated mansion in the Highlands and attempted to restore it as a home for the extended family, was told in a gripping television series in 2004 and in the media thereafter. When the Dobsons sold up, at least partly defeated by the scale of the building, they may have made a financial profit, but it could be argued that they also paid a high price in the fracturing and severing of close family relationships, and the intrusively intimate public portrayal of their troubles by the media.

The large and complex buildings are in the minority, though. The reason that most of the recently restored castles are small and relatively straightforward in architectural terms is that they were abandoned by their owners in the seventeenth and eighteenth centuries as being just that: too small, and also too old fashioned and too inconvenient for modern living at the time. Examples of long-abandoned and ruined sixteenth-century towers that were restored in the twentieth and twenty-first centuries are Barholm and Tilquhillie. The McCullochs of Barholm abandoned the tower at some time in the middle of the eighteenth century and moved to a large Adam mansion, Barholm House, which they had built 5 miles away. It was demolished in the 1960s.

The Interiors

However traumatic the building work may have been, most owners at least enjoy the task of fitting out and furnishing the interiors of their newly restored castles. Scouring salesrooms, auction houses and antique stores for furniture that will look well in a sixteenth-century interior is the fun part of what is usually a long and exhausting process. Queen Marie furnished her restored castle, Castle Bran, with traditional Romanian crafts and artefacts, in the same way that many restorers in Scotland favour tartan and Scottish Jacobean furniture.

The restorer of Rusco Tower, Graham Carson, took great pride in the sourcing of materials – including second-hand stone from the platform of Leuchars railway junction and seasoned yellow pine from a demolished church organ in Edinburgh. In Ballencrieff a chair in one of the guest bedrooms was a gift from Nigel Tranter, who helped Peter Gillies to find his castle and advised on the restoration. Ballencrieff has so many rooms, including seven bedrooms, that Peter had the luxury of leaving the Great Hall, with its magnificently re-plastered Renaissance ceiling, completely empty apart from a grand piano and a settle, showing off the space to great effect.

James Brown's plans for the restoration of Baltersan included detailed specifications of the interior when advertising for sponsors. The description on the website was enticing:

The whole property will be decorated, furnished and fitted to very high standards, including original works of art and antiques, respecting the historic fabric and acknowledging the hierarchy of the building. The entrancing visual delights of Renaissance architecture; the smell of leather-bound books, wood fires and beeswax candles; the gentle touch of smooth, limewashed plaster and heavy, damask drapes; the secure sound of strong, iron keys turning in sturdy locks and thick, oak doors firmly closing; the taste of fresh, organic food and that sixth sense – that can only be felt by the individual.

We lived in Holland while we were restoring Barholm and I had great fun in Dutch 'snuffel' markets, snuffling out bargains. Holland had not yet been hit with the wave of television programmes encouraging viewers to hunt out incredible bargains in car-boot sales and to make money from selling their unwanted old goods at auction. Yet second-hand goods sales were enormously popular, with a huge range on offer very, very cheaply. I was looking mainly for pewter, copper and old rugs from the Middle East, which I found quite often for remarkably good prices. There must have been a fashion for pewter jugs and plates in Holland in the 1960s, since so many were for sale among other items from

Interior at Aiket Tower (Courtesy of Rober Clow)

Re-enactment at Buittle Tower

that era. A set of heavy, pewter measuring jugs cost 5 euros. A vast and extremely solid copper cauldron pot in excellent condition was 20 euros. A large, old, copper jelly mould was only 1 euro. In addition, I picked up all sorts of unusual odds and ends, such as old wooden speculaas (a kind of Dutch gingerbread) moulds and several intricately carved models of spinning wheels. I started collecting old, blue and white tiles at between 5–10 euros each and ended up with hundreds, some of which now look very fitting as they wind up the spiral staircase. Others might look good lining the fireplace in our bedroom if we can sort them into a suitable set and find a skilled tiler who will position and grout them safely.

The Grounds and Gardens

Most ruined castles were sold with large gardens of up to 5 acres, rather than policies or estates. Of these, the majority were sold with between 1 and 5 acres, while thirteen had less than 1 acre. The amount of land sold with a ruined castle did not represent the estate in which the building would once have been situated, but often seemed to be just the smallest amount that the seller could reasonably offer. Farmers and landowners, who represent most of

LANG MAY SHE LIVE
AND LANG BE LOVED;
AND LANG MAY SHE BE HAPPY

Our Scottish Queen

GLAMIS CASTLE.
The Home of H.M.Queen Elizabeth.

Postcard depicting the Queen Mother and Glamis Castle

the sellers, do not give up land lightly. The outbuildings and walled enclosures that once would have surrounded the towers and castles had nearly all disappeared, with the notable exception of Buittle Tower, whose restoring owners, Janet and Jeffrey Burn, regularly stage exciting historical re-enactments in their outbuildings.

Only one of the castles sold with more than 50 acres of land – Fordell – was restored solely or primarily as a family home. The rest were used as the holiday homes of wealthy owners (Balmuto, Barscobe, Castle of Mey, Harthill) for building development (Sundrum), or they incorporated businesses (Comlongon and Midmar). Subsequent owners sometimes sought to buy back enough land to situate their castle within a larger acreage, for example Robert Clow of Aiket Castle in Ayrshire, who planted 7,000 trees on his additional acres, John Coyne in Tilquhillie, and Sue and Ian Brash of Fa'side, near Edinburgh. At Barholm we bought the wooded ravine behind the castle from the neighbouring farmer and have developed a sheltered woodland garden and fernery there. The owner of Niddry Castle has tried to buy the castle's walled garden from the estate in which it stands, without success. The Clan Menzies Trust did manage to buy back Castle Menzies' walled garden in 1984, then in a sorry state, and have done some restoration work, repairing the central staircase and clearing the terraces. At the start of the twentieth century, ten full-time gardeners would have been employed, and now there is only volunteer labour, but the Menzies Charitable Trust is doing its best to keep the garden tidy.

Only a few of the restored castles have a walled or enclosed garden, among them Pitcullo, Liberton House, Barholm, Midmar, Ochiltree, Buittle, Spedlins, and Glenapp. All of these are well maintained, although not necessarily in the charming Renaissance style employed at Ochiltree Tower and Liberton House, which sets off the buildings so beautifully. Gardening in Scotland is a constant battle against the weather, but the Castle of Mey, one of the most northerly castles in Scotland, nevertheless manages to produce a wide variety of fruit and vegetables within the high garden walls, all chosen for their resistance to wind and sea spray. Raspberries, strawberries, gooseberries, apples, currants, potatoes, peas, beans, carrots, turnips, onions and leeks all thrive.

Eilean Donan, Scotland's most iconic castle (Photo by David Iliff. License: CC–BY–SA 3.0)

Balmoral Castle

Interior of Blackhall Manor in Paisley

The painted ceiling at Barholm Castle

Kelburn Castle near Glasgow with graffiti art

Interior at Newmilns Tower

Tilquhillie Castle in Aberdeenshire

Liberton Tower in Edinburgh

Burg Rheinstein in Germany,
restored by Prince Frederick
of Prussia, 1825 (© Manfred
Heyde. License: CC–BY–SA 3.0)

Old Place of Mochrum
in Wigtownshire,
restored in 1873

Castle Bran,
'Dracula's castle'
in Romania
(© Florin73m. License:
CC–BY–SA 3.0)

Earlshall Castle in Fife,
restored by Robert
Lorimer in 1891

Torthorwald Castle in Dumfriesshire – a sadly decaying ruin in the landscape

Hallway at Ochiltree Castle, Midlothian

Interior of Brackenhill Tower near
Longtown, Cumbria

Jeffrey Burn, restorer of
Buittle Tower

Archers at Buittle Tower, Kirkudbrightshire

Liberton House in Edinburgh

Parterre at Ochiltree Castle

Fa'side Castle,
East Lothian

Tilquhillie Castle bedroom

Terpersie Castle in Aberdeenshire (Courtesy of Richard Paxman)

Glenapp Castle in Ayrshire

Balbithan Castle in Aberdeenshire

Interior of Tillycairn Castle, Aberdeenshire

Castle Stalker in Argyll

Graham Carson, restorer of Rusco Tower in Kirkcudbrightshire (Courtesy of Josh Carson)

Duart Castle on the Isle of Mull, restored in 1911

Kisimul Castle in
the Outer Hebrides
(Courtesy of
Mats Ljungberg)

Barscobe Castle in Kirkcudbrightshire

Borthwick Castle, Midlothian

Castle Leslie, Aberdeenshire
(Courtesy of Richard Paxman)

CHAPTER 3

THE RESTORERS

What kind of people restored Scottish castles? In many ways, the restoring owners are as different and individual as their castles. But there are a few readily categorised (and not mutually exclusive) groups – for example, the 'family heritage' restorers, the architects, the do-it-yourself types and the entrepreneurs. The question of what motivated them is an interesting one. It is clear from the many stories of hardships and battles that castle restoration is a difficult and risky business, particularly for the less affluent. Why, then, do people do it? Are they 'a bit mad' as Stuart Morris of Balgonie claims? This is the view of some onlookers. 'Is the man deranged?' asked Tom Clarke's son-in-law when he heard that his wife's father had bought a second ruin, Kilmartin, for restoration. 'All our friends thought we were barking mad. It was just a pile of masonry. We had to have nerves of steel!' said Lachlan Stewart about Ballone. Judy Steel claimed that 'although we might be regarded as mad to embark on the restoration of Aikwood, there were people far madder than us, who had tackled completely roofless, empty shells and made them into homes'. Madness, or at least a serious lack of caution, may be one driving force behind the restorers, and it appears in lots of media reports and narratives.

However, when asked to articulate their motivations, the restorers mostly reflect rather carefully to explain why they should take on a huge and challenging building project. Some wanted to be a part of history and feel the continuity. 'One of the best things about a place like this is that you feel like you are living and breathing history ... Just by being here, I feel I'm part of a continuing saga,' said Malin Nairn of Niddry. Gillian Clarke, of Kirkhope Tower, talked of legacy as an incentive: 'You rush about all your life and perhaps don't make much impact. Kirkhope's restoration will be a small mark that we leave for the future.' Peter Hewkin of Craigrownie Castle identified altruism, plus an obsession with the challenge, as being part of his motivation. In his late 40s, he had spent his working life in property investment and wanted, as he put it, 'to give something back to the world'.

Others were touched by the neglect and decay they observed in the ruins. Jeremy Irons, restorer of Kilcoe in Ireland, looked with sadness on how it had been ignored and vandalised over the centuries, how the carved window stones had been pushed out and robbed, and how one particular part was near to collapse. Tim Erbe, who bought and extensively repaired Logie Elphinstone, said simply, 'it saddened me that this prominent historic house was sitting there, in danger of crumbling away, needing put back together again.' The 'putting back together' of something broken is another theme identified by some restorers: 'This desire to repair, restore and to make things work is a strong motivating force. It therefore is logical that I might consider refurbishing a house, particularly if it was a ruin, and, being romantics at heart, my wife Claire and I decided to restore a tower house.'[27] Tom Craig of Fa'side referred, in the preceding quote, to being 'romantics at heart' and this kind of vision of the self, and of a medieval revivalism, was echoed by Judy Corbett in her autobiographical account of the restoration of Gwydir Castle in Wales:

> We harboured a dream of one day buying a ruinous old mansion and renovating it as accurately as possible and living in it without electricity or any concessions to modern life. My dream was to wear a chatelaine round my waist, and keep wolfhounds and tend bees in some quiet corner of a walled garden. I had a strong sense of the Gothic in me, and neglected houses, in particular, appealed to something deep within my psyche.[28]

The romantic dream motive crops up frequently. Lachlan Rhodes spoke of his motivations for buying and restoring Terpersie in Aberdeenshire:

> My mother was brought up in a Scottish castle; I've always been a romantic and visited many of the ruined castles of Scotland. I was bought a Castles of Scotland map at university and used that to see the remarkable array of castles and tower houses across Scotland. In particular, the restoration of Tillycairn in Aberdeenshire inspired me. I manoeuvered friends to get me invited to a party where I could meet up with Ian Fellowes-Gordon, who then owned Terpersie, and fortunately it was just at the time he had decided to sell. I put in an offer and bought the place for a very modest sum.

Nicholas Browne, like the owners of Rusco, Ballone, Kisimul and Mains, bought a castle as a kind of dream fulfilment: 'As a small boy I dreamed that one day I'd live in a castle, with a winding stone stair, battlements and turrets.'[29] Graham Cowan, on the other hand, had had no initial dream but was taken by surprise, ambushed almost, at the impact of Glenapp Castle when he first saw it: 'It was a completely breathtaking sight – a forgotten place – a sleeping beauty, like the castle in the fairytale that slept for a hundred years.'

Matthew Parris, too, had not been looking for a restoration project when he found l'Avenc in Spain, but 'there was something different about this place: something enchanted. It hit you between the eyes.'[30] Peter Clarke seemed to perceive his ruin as a youthful alternative to romance or sex: 'I fell in love with Kirkhope immediately. I was only 18 and hadn't discovered girls yet. It was just a pile of old rubble at the time, but I thought it was the most beautiful and breathtaking thing I'd ever seen.' A couple of owners looked to the future, one being Peter Gillies of Ballencrieff: 'When doing a restoration like this, you will either finish it or it will finish you,' he says. 'You need to have vision and you need to be prepared to work years ahead of yourself.' James Brown also implied that this was important, although in his case, sadly, the vision never came to fruition: 'I have been asked on many occasions what motivated me to pursue the saving of this wonderful historic building. My answer has been simple, "because I can see what it could become".'

Lairds and Ladies

One aspect of castle representation that is particularly salient for Scottish castle owners is the 'lairdly' one. The title of 'laird' is so significant that several new owners who have obtained the title with their castle use it as part of their identity in daily life. The use of the title of 'laird' by a new purchaser is allowable, when one considers that a Scottish feudal barony can be sold with the land (or could, until the Abolition of Feudal Tenure (Scotland) Act of 2000 came into force). This may be one great attraction to some purchasers of a Scottish castle as they gain instant membership into the titled classes, sometimes to the amused disdain or even outrage of the 'real' gentry, who may ostracise the newcomers. The Earl of Bradford became so distressed by the sale of fake titles that he set up a website (www.faketitles.com) entitled on the home page, 'The site that lifts the lid', to warn people against purchasing them on the Internet. If you should wish to do so, the owners of Dunans Castle sell a limitless number of titles on the Internet from only £39, in order to fund their restoration, which seems a harmless enough pursuit. Referring to a sale of Irish hereditary titles, James Charles Roy, the American restorer of Moyode Castle in Ireland, confessed:

> My wife and I sat around mocking the poor, status-seeking dodos who would buy such decadent scraps of snobbery for thousands of dollars, but what I didn't dare reveal was that I could be tempted. Baron of Moyode? It has a nice ring to it, and let's face it, a coat of arms would do wonders for my otherwise pedestrian calling cards.[31]

It is not only the 'common man' that can be seduced by a title; when Nicholas Fairbairn, who was a prominent solicitor and QC, and later an MP and Solicitor General for Scotland, acquired Fordell Castle, near Dunfermline, he styled himself Baron Fairbairn of Fordell, although his claim never went to the heraldic court of Lord Lyon for verification. The previous owner of Barholm Castle, who had hoped to restore it from its ruinous state, called himself the Baron of Barholm, but we have found no evidence that such a title goes with the property.

Female Restorers

Whichever group one looks at, there are very few women, however. Restorers, castellologists, researchers, conservation architects and authors who write on castle-related themes are overwhelmingly represented by men. Only four women have been the sole purchasers and restorers of castles – the first was the Queen Mother (Castle of Mey), who grew up living in castles.

Helen Bailey was, unusually, a self-made woman, who poured her savings into the restoration of Borthwick Castle. Alexa Scott-Plummer restored a number of historic buildings, including Lanton Tower in the Borders and Mary McMurtrie bought and restored Balbithan Castle, then set up a nursery garden business within the grounds, after being widowed at an early age.

Extraordinarily, Gillian Strickland won Powrie Castle in Angus as a prize in a competition run by the National Trust for Scotland, by suggesting the best plan for its future. She had just married the politician Peter Clarke, so they restored part of the castle as a couple. Later, in 1994, they restored Kirkhope Tower in the Borders, and lived in it until her premature death in 2013. Indeed, the majority of purchasers are married couples, although the narratives have almost exclusively been told by the husbands, via books and media articles, with wives cast in a supporting role. The only exceptions are Judy Steel of Aikwood and Judy Corbett, who restored Gwydir Castle in Wales with her husband, both of whom wrote accounts of their restoration projects. Judy Corbett's book, *Castles in the Air: The Restoration Adventures of Two Young Optimists and a Crumbling Old Mansion*, is a thrilling adventure story and received plenty of critical acclaim when it was published in 2005.

Lady Steel receiving an award for the restoration of Aikwood Tower

Yeats' wife was given no credit for her part in the restoration of Thoor Ballylee; in his poem (*See* Chapter 7) he claimed that he 'restored the tower for my wife George'. 'But the poem's truth conceals another, and different truth – that they worked together at the restoration, and it was largely her vision and hands that created a dwelling from the former ruins.'[32]

Although women do not feature prominently in the Scottish castle restoration literature and narratives, several independently wealthy women have 'saved' Scottish castles in various ways. In the 1950s, Margaret Udny-Hamilton demolished the Victorian baronial extension at Udny Castle and carried out renovation work on the original tower. Margaret Sempill-Forbes bought back Druminnor, or Forbes Castle, in the late

1950s and executed a similar project there. Hope MacDougall, owner of Gylen Castle, commissioned architect, Martin Hadlington, to consolidate the ruin in the 1990s (backed by a generous grant from Historic Scotland and funds raised by clan members). In 1989–90, Alexa Scott-Plummer, with architect Philip Mercer, radically changed and renovated Lanton Tower in the Borders, and then in the early 1990s spent six years repairing and renovating Cowdenknowes House, which incorporates a sixteenth-century tower, with Andrew Davey of Simpson and Brown architects. The wealthy 'Stagecoach' transport entrepreneur, Ann Gloag, bought two large Scottish nineteenth-century castles: Beaufort in 1994, which was sold to help pay off Lord Lovat's inheritance tax, and Kinfauns in 2004, although they needed refurbishment rather than restoration.

Out of more than 300 books and academic articles about castles consulted for this book, more than 95 per cent were written by men. This may simply be a

Tillycairn Castle

reflection of the gender divide in almost every area of history, although castles are even more starkly gendered than most topics in a largely male-dominated subject. The photograph on page 69 shows Judy Steel in front of Aikwood Tower with the restoration team, which consisted of twenty-six men and no women – although she was the overall project manager.

The 'Family Heritage' Restorers

A dozen family heritage restorers bought back the family estate – or were at least buying a ruined castle with the same name as their family name. For them, there was a sense of mission bound up with identity, sometimes at the level of family and sometimes at the level of clan. Lineage is an important concept to the members of this group. Their financial resources varied, but most worked

physically on their building, presumably to 'cement' their relationship with it in a very personal way. The majority also acted as their own master of works, supervising the project. They are:

Major Nicholas McLean-Bristol
    — Breachacha
Robert Lister Macneil — Kisimul
Graham Carson — Rusco

Charles Stuart — Castle Stuart
David Leslie — Castle Leslie
David Lumsden — Tillycairn
Major Roy Armstrong-Wilson —
  Gilknockie (aka Hollows Tower),
  now housing the
  Clan Armstrong centre
Roderick Oliphant — Hatton
Lt-Col D.R. Stewart Allward
  — Castle Stalker
Harry Boswell — Balmuto
Lieutenant General Sir George Gordon
  Lennox — Gordon Castle

To take the last-mentioned first, Frederick Gordon Lennox, the 9th Duke of Richmond and 4th of Gordon, sold Gordon Castle and his Scottish estates in 1938 as a result of death duties following the passing of his father and grandfather. The castle fell into disrepair, but was bought back by one of the 7th duke's other grandsons, Lieutenant General Sir George Gordon Lennox, after the Second World War. He was forced to knock much of it down due to significant dry and wet rot, but then turned it into the family home it is today. His son, Major General Bernard Gordon Lennox continued to live there with his wife, Sally-Rose, and now his grandson has taken over the running of Gordon Castle and Estate.

David Lumsden and Tillycairn

Tillycairn is a sixteenth-century, five-storey tower in Aberdeenshire. The castle was built in 1550 by Matthew Lumsden and was a derelict ruin for over 250 years, after being destroyed by fire in 1722. It was restored by David

Installation of new windows into Lord Perth's fifteenth-century private chapel at Stobhall Castle in 2004 (Courtesy of Rab MacInnes and Linda Cannon)

Lumsden of Cushnie, who held the heraldic title of Garioch Pursuivant to the Chief of the Name and Arms of Mar; he was also president of the Scottish Military History Society and convener of the Monarchist League of Scotland. Having already restored Cushnie House, built in 1688 by Alexander Lumsden, in 1980, David Lumsden began the restoration of Tillycairn. The restoration, which involved the sorting and removal of hundreds of years' worth of rubble, took four years. The character and architectural integrity of the original structure with rounded corners, circular staircase tower and corbelled cylindrical turrets, was retained and Tillycairn Castle became a comfortable seven-bedroom family home, which has changed hands a couple of times since the 1980s. David Lumsden went on to restore Leithen Lodge at Innerleithen – a grandiose, 1880s shooting lodge in the Borders. He then set up the Castles of Scotland Preservation Trust in conjunction with the late Lord Borthwick, Nigel Tranter and Hugh Ross, and, in the 1990s, he oversaw the restoration of Liberton Tower in Edinburgh on behalf of the Trust.

Lt-Col. D.R. Stewart Allward and Castle Stalker

Situated on a tiny tidal island on Loch Linnhe in Argyll, Castle Stalker is a picturesque fifteenth-century fortified tower. King James IV, who was a cousin of the Stewarts of Appin, is said to have stayed there often, using it as a hunting base. Ownership of the castle fluctuated over the centuries between the Stewarts and the Campbells, in a series of often-violent struggles, until it was abandoned by the Campbells in about 1840. In 1908, it was regained from the Campbells by Charles Stewart of Achara who bought it and carried out some basic preservation work to stem its decay. In 1947, his successor, Duncan Stewart, who was Governor of Sarawak, was murdered and the castle devolved on his widow. In 1965, Lt-Col. D.R. Stewart Allward bought the castle from her and spent the next ten years rebuilding and restoring it to a habitable state. The restoration was carried out by Lt-Col. Stewart Allward personally with the help of his wife, family and many friends who were willing to spend holidays and long weekends helping with the task. It is open for a limited number of tours each year.

Robert Lister Macneil and Kisimul

Kisimul is a rare surviving medieval castle in the Western Isles, situated on a tiny islet off the island of Barra. It had been burned out in 1795 and much of the stone removed and/or destroyed in the nineteenth century. Kisimul was owned by the Macneils until 1838, when it was sold to pay off debts. Robert Lister Macneil, an American architect who had been officially recognised as the Chief of the Clan Macneil by the Lord Lyon in 1915, managed to buy the Barra Estate and Kisimul Castle in 1937 from the estate of Lady Cathcart (who had refused to sell to him during her lifetime, despite his persistent pleading), with the help of his second wife's money and clan donations. Robert Lister saw the acquisition of Kisimul as part of his destiny, his boyhood dream and his life's goal. The repair and restoration of Kisimul began in 1937, but the work was interrupted by the Second World War. The restoration proper began in 1957; the story was told by Robert Lister Macneil in the last chapter of his book, *Castle in the Sea*. He drew his own master plan for the castle and had blueprints drawn up in 1938. 'I did think of Kisimul as if I were going to awaken it from a long sleep and give it renewed life, a secure life which would continue through future centuries and, I hoped, make the castle pleasurable and inspiring to many generations.'[33]

In 1956, just before the restoration work began, Macneil received a royal visit, which would doubtless have compounded his sense of the importance of his project. Queen Elizabeth, the Duke of Edinburgh and Princess Margaret came to Kisimul on 14 August:

> The Queen and the Duke asked my wife and myself many questions about Kisimul Castle. The Duke asked me what I intended to do with the castle and I told him 'I hope to live in it, if I live long enough, and to make it the clan centre.' He replied by asking me if I knew about Maclean of Duart, who started restoration of his castle when he was about seventy and lived in it until he was nearly one hundred and one years old. I said I was trying to equal Maclean of Duart's record.[34]

Despite Macneil's plan for longevity at Kisimul, Michael Davis claimed that was not a practicality: 'Scarcely intended for modern occupation and certainly not suited to it, Kisimul was simply patched up and some domestic buildings within the courtyard were rebuilt for occasional residence.'[35] Macneil's story is a 'ripping yarn', with elements of heritage, clan continuity, Highland welcome, dramatic rescue, battling the elements and visiting royalty. It represents adventure and romance, 'boyhood dreams come true' and must have been a truly inspiring read for interested Macneil clan members in the 1960s. Unfortunately, Macneil of Barra was badly advised over the restoration of Kisimul by the Ministry of Works, who referred him to a reinforced concrete supply company. As RCAHMS admitted forty-five years later: 'The 20th century rebuild was largely conjectural, making liberal use of concrete and cement render.' Historic Scotland took over responsibility for managing and conserving Kisimul in 2000, signing a 999-year lease from Ian Roderick Macneil, 46th Clan Chief, for £1 and an annual rent of a bottle of Talisker whisky. In 2013, members of Clan Macneil and Historic Scotland raised £200,000 for further conservation and archaeological work.

The Earl of Perth and Stobhall

The Earl of Perth bought Stobhall Castle in 1953 from the Earl of Ancaster, who had intended to give it to the nation after inheriting it. David Perth and his American wife, Nancy, began the long-term restoration of Stobhall as a labour of love, while he was working in the City of London. The Dower House was riddled with wet and dry rot and had to be almost gutted and re-roofed, leaving only the stone staircase and its wonderful plaster ceiling. They built a passage connecting the Dower House to the kitchen. Later, in 1965, they built the library on the site of a pair of earlier decrepit cottages. Massive work was required to stabilise the courtyard because the Pend and burn-side wall were slipping into the den. However, although the Earl of Perth devoted himself to the restoration of Stobhall and lived there until his death at the age of 95, the quality of the work that he oversaw was poor, partly because of bad advice and partly because of financial constraints as the costs of the restoration rose. When the castle was taken over by his grandson, in 2004, the latter began a necessary renewal of the original restoration, with replacements of many of the window surrounds, crow-steps, chimneys and other stonework – largely because of

Doorway and armorial panel at
Barscobe Castle

the advice in the 1950s by the Ministry of Works to use hard, non-porous cement for the repointing.

In 2012, Stobhall was sold and the contents auctioned by Bonhams, raising over £900,000, after the grandson, James Drummond, Viscount Strathallan, decided to move to London. The castle was put up for sale at £2.35 million, described by estate agents as being set in a 196-acre woodland site, with six double and four single bedrooms, seven bathrooms, a music room, library, chapel, lodge house, folly, staff flat, garages, gardens, duck flighting pond and adjacent Campsie Island.

Major Nicholas Maclean-Bristol and Breachacha

Breachacha Castle is a large fifteenth- to seventeenth-century stronghold on the Island of Coll in the Western Isles, which had been ruinous since 1750 when Major Maclean-Bristol bought it in 1961.

Like Robert Lister-Macneil, Nicholas Maclean-Bristol had had a childhood vision of buying back the family castle. His great-grandfather thirteen times removed had built Breachacha, which was sold out of the family in 1856, and Nicholas Maclean-Bristol had decided, at the age of 8, that he would buy it back one day. He did so, aged 21. This is Maclean's description of his first visit to Coll in the early 1960s:

> The weather was good and the Island was magical. I decided that this was where I wanted to spend my life. Hughie also took me to see the Castle. It stood gaunt, roofless and empty. No one had lived in it since 1750; apart from my family no one had ever lived there; it had never been blown up or burnt down; it had just decayed quietly like an old warrior once his active life was over. But was Breacachadh's use over? Could it be restored? I knew of Sir Fitzroy Maclean's restoration of Duart and MacNeill of Barra's at Kishmul. I decided that I would take on the third restoration of a medieval Hebridean castle. Kenneth Stewart, who had inherited the Coll estate, and who I met on my first visit to the Island, was prepared to sell Breacachadh Castle to me and shortly after I became ADC it became mine.[36]

Duart Castle was also mentioned in the account of Kisimul's restoration. Sir Fitzroy Maclean had been determined to purchase and restore Duart since a family holiday to Scotland in the 1870s. In 1911, he finally achieved his aim and bought the ruined castle and 300 acres from Mrs Guthrie,

the widow of Mr Murray Guthrie, who had inherited the estate from an uncle. Maclean-Bristol might also have mentioned Col. MacRae Gilstrap, who restored Eilean Donan with the help of a rich wife's money from 1912–32.

These four restorations (Duart, Kisimul, Eilean Donan and Breachacha) sit apart in the world of castle restorations in their focus on clan continuity and the regaining of a Highland birth right. Their buildings, too, were different from the simple towers that comprised the majority of individual restorations, being older and much more complex in their construction history.

> Since I bought Breacachadh I had been trying to work out what I would do with it. Certainly I wanted it to be the home for my wife and children if and when I got married, but I also saw it as the centre of an international organization. I knew from my study of Maclean history that many Collachs, who had gone overseas, had been remarkably successful. They had first left as mercenary soldiers, then as colonists and finally as soldiers in the British army. Was there something in Coll's environment that could inspire a new generation in Britain to serve overseas, and return to enrich their own communities?[37]

As well as a vision of family continuity, like Macneil of Kisimul, Nicholas Maclean-Bristol had another vision for the future, a vision that he realised through setting up Project Trust in 1967; an educational charity that sends young people overseas to work as volunteers alongside needy communities and to learn from them. Between 1967 and 2007, almost 6,000 young people worked in over fifty countries. All had to go to Coll for an initial selection course and a debriefing, and in the early years, before additional accommodation was built, they lodged in Breachacha Castle with Nicholas Maclean-Bristol and his wife, Lavinia. This is, I believe, the only example of an individual restoring owner dedicating the castle for good in the community, involving a charitable educational purpose.

Graham Carson and Rusco

In the mid-1960s, Graham Carson decided that he would act upon his childhood dream of living in a castle and pursue an ambition to restore a Scottish tower house. 'Like many wee boys. I had been fascinated by castles, but unlike some, I had never grown out of this fascination and by my mid-twenties I was day-dreaming about restoring one when I retired.'[38] He spoke to Nigel Tranter, a modest man, who suggested that Graham should consult his five volumes of *The Fortified Tower House* in the local library. Having gallantly purchased the books, Graham drew up a shortlist of eleven towers. Rusco Tower is a small, fifteenth-century tower that originally stood on land owned by John Accarson, so he was especially delighted that he would be bringing back the Carson name to Rusco. In 1972, long before his retirement, Graham persuaded the reluctant owners to sell the ruined tower, with 11 acres around it, by making the risky but attractive offer of giving back the building for nothing if he had not completed the restoration by a specified date. The Carsons then spent three years on the planning applications and carried out the restoration over a period of four years, although there were many challenges along the way and two periods when work had to stop completely for lack of funds. Their meticulous restoration was honoured with a Saltire Society Award. Graham discovered that a barony came with the tower, and subsequently had the baronial arms moulded in plaster above the Great Hall fireplace, 'literally plastering his achievement' as he put it.

Graham acted as his own clerk of works, organising and supervising the workforce. Like the Murdoch family at Methven, the Carsons all pitched in for some heavy work:

> The only job at which the whole Carson family soiled their hands was that of de-slating a roof – and dirty work it really was! ... The heaviest was about three quarters of a hundredweight and they had to be handed down carefully, from person to person from off the roof, using two ladders.

Graham's own involvement in the rebuilding work was very hands-on, and not without its comic elements.

This is his account of clearing out the tower, which, like many other ruins, had been used as part of the farm buildings:

> The cows had been using the building as a house of ease for I don't know how long, and the floor was eighteen inches deep in rich manure. So my first job was to start clearing it. I hired an enormous great pump and it worked manfully for fully an hour and a half. I was standing up to my knees in rotting manure. Suddenly there was the most almighty bang, followed by a hissing noise. I rushed outside. Oh dear! There was what was left of the large pump, with its contents scattered everywhere![39]

As the owner of a kilt-making business, Graham always wore the kilt; a combination of the kilted owner, barony and the castle made a nice lairdly image. Looking back on the restoration, he said: 'The most rewarding part of having undertaken all the work has been the change in the quality of our life, despite the uncompromising nature of the building. We feel very privileged to be custodians of something which stood for nearly 500 years, and we hope that, with a little help from us and our successors, it will do the same again.' In 2006, the Carsons passed the ownership of Rusco Tower to their son and moved to a more convenient house nearby.

The Menzies Clan Society and Castle Menzies

The Menzies Clan Society bought the derelict Castle Menzies in 1957 for less than £300. For the next fourteen years it was visited by Clan Society members at the annual clan gathering, but was in too dangerous a condition to allow access to the general public. In 1971, surveys indicated that urgent work was needed and plans were made for restoration of the sixteenth-century part, aided by a grant from the Historic Buildings Council (now Historic Scotland) and fundraising. The whole restoration, including the Victorian wing, took forty years and was largely achieved due to the energetic input of Dr Bill Dewar and his wife, Ann. Now Castle Menzies is a successful weddings and events venue, and is used by the Clan Society for meetings and to house a library.

DIY Restorers and Wealthy Second-Homeowners

The new restoring owners represent a wide range of professions, levels of income and degrees of knowledge and understanding about historic buildings, but the majority were on some kind of a budget, some very tight.

Most had enough resources to employ an architect, at least to draw up plans for them, and some professional help. The majority, rich or not, were in some way directly involved in the rebuilding (one exception being Barholm, as we were living overseas, although we tackled the field of hogweed and thistles surrounding the tower every time we visited, gradually turning it into a rather nice garden). All of the restorers had to employ tradesmen and labourers to help to a greater or lesser extent, but several, like Gerald Laing at Kinkell, worked alongside their workforce throughout the rebuilding. Other new owners, with jobs and commitments that prevented them working full time on their restorations, nevertheless acted as their own project managers and directed the work; among these, most participated in at least some of the unskilled building tasks. 'There's something about smacking your own thumb now and again, shedding blood on your own roof, that gives you perspective and shapes a desire for perfection. Doing for yourself also arms you for encounters with other builders less careful or scrupulous.'[40]

Mains Castle, near East Kilbride, is a fifteenth-century tower, which was bought in a ruinous condition from a local farmer in 1976 for £150 by Mike Rowan, an entertainer by profession (the kilted, stilt performer Big Rory), and a DIY restorer on a tight budget. It seemed that until he approached the farmer, no one had been interested in the castle. Mike enjoyed showing visitors a cutting from a newspaper dated 1952, which describes the crumbling nature of the castle, and predicted: 'It is likely to fall away completely. Yet the fabric is still perfectly good, and would well repay renovation into a very manageable present-day homestead by some person of good taste and discrimination.'

The story of Mike Rowan's restoration of Mains Castle was broadcast as a television programme in the 1970s, which doubtless encouraged others to fantasise about doing the same. His account is one of adventure, dream fulfilment, financial difficulties and physical hardship:

> While we were restoring the castle, we lived in a beautiful Edwardian caravan, with cut-glass windows. Our friends thought it was dead romantic, but it was a freezingly cold existence. After two extremely snowy winters, it was a blessing, but only a blessing in disguise, to move into an equally cold tower house![41]

The military aspects of restorers' castles feature in many accounts, representing a fascination with defensiveness. An entire page of Mike Rowan's account is given over to the defensive properties of the tower, with a discussion of gunloops, bows and arrows and sword-sharpening marks. He was determined 'to restore the castle without compromise, using traditional materials and finishes, wherever possible'.[42]

This initially included bare stone walls, which he saw as being particularly 'Scots' (Ranald MacInnes identified 'rubblemania' as having a seductive appeal to many modern castle owners, despite its historical inauthenticity). 'However, I changed my mind and plastered the bedroom, leaving the window surrounds with an exposed four inch margin of stone. It is a real treat to sit in the embrasure and I must admit that the rooms are so much better for being plastered.'[43] As, indeed, they almost certainly were originally, in their truly authentic state.

Mike Rowan's castle restoration, like so many others, was a form of boyhood wish fulfilment: 'When I was eight I crawled through a small hole in the walls of the ruins of Mearns Castle, Glasgow (which is still a ruin and on the Buildings at Risk Register), and from that moment I began to dream that one day I would have a castle of my own!' Having used the Great Hall for corporate entertaining events involving venison cooked on a peat fire, bagpipes and whisky in order to fund the upkeep, Mike Rowan sold Mains Castle in 1998, twenty-two years after buying and restoring it. The woman who bought the property from him planned to use it as restaurant and tourist attraction, but was unable to do so due to planning regulations and had to sell up again in 2001.

However, in addition to the DIY restorers on a tight budget, several

Castle Leslie by MacGibbon and Ross (*c.* 1890)

wealthy restorers purchased a ruined castle to restore it for use as a second or holiday home. These consisted of owners, like the Queen Mother, who could readily afford to have the work carried out by a professional team of architects and builders and who paid them to get on with the job, rather than becoming directly involved in the work themselves. Sir Hugh Wontner, chairman of the Savoy Hotel Group and of the Savoy Theatre and Lord Mayor of London, bought the estate on which the ruinous Barscobe Castle stood in 1961, having rented Barscobe House as a holiday home in previous years. He decided to restore the seventeenth-century tower and was advised in his restoration project by Dame Bridget D'Oyly Carte, who was the first tenant once the restoration was finished and who lived there until her death in 1985. Although he took no physical part in the restoration of Barscobe, every year Sir Hugh would take a paintbrush and ceremoniously repaint the armorial arms above the front door, indicating an urge for some 'hands-on' involvement with the building, if only at a symbolic level.

The second restorer of Law Castle (the first had had the building repossessed before finishing), the entrepreneur David Hutton, was in the lucky position of not having to count costs. In an interview with the *Observer* he said, 'The restoration wasn't too stressful – it was good fun. Fortunately, I'm in a position where money isn't a problem, and profit wasn't a goal. I think you have to have that point of view if you try to plan such a big, unpredictable project.' Robert Pooley of Forter Castle is reported to have spent £1 million in 1990, equivalent to almost £2 million in 2013, restoring Forter Castle, a small sixteenth-century tower, from a ruinous state.

Nicholas Fairbairn and Fordell Castle

Fordell Castle dates from the sixteenth century and is the only example of a tower house with two main stairs, each with its own door to the outside. It was bought in 1961 by Nicholas Fairbairn (1933–1995), a flamboyant and controversial solicitor, sometime Solicitor-General for Scotland and Scottish Tory politician. It was inhabited at the time by a woman whom Fairbairn described as an 'inebriated chatelaine'. In 1961 Fordell was 'half-constructed, half-dilapidated' and a 'slum', but it did have a roof and internal walls, floors and ceilings. Fairbairn moved in immediately after his wedding to Elizabeth MacKay. He gave over ten pages in his autobiography, *A Life is Too Short*, to a narrative of his restoration of Fordell Castle, in which he, like Robert Macneil of Kisimul, conveys a sense of adventure and a fight against the elements. It is not clear whether Fairbairn himself was physically involved in the building work, despite his use of 'we'. He expresses his lack of prescience in this quote:

Had I known the extent of the task of the resurrection on which I was embarking, I would perhaps never have undertaken it at all, but is that not true of all in life? ... And so the great work continued, sometimes fast and sometime slowly. The final event was the pointing of the outside. We erected scaffolding – in a high wind I remember – and pointed the whole exterior. It was a daunting task, but it had its reward in completion; I never want to erect scaffolding again, and I pay my tribute to those who erect and work on it ... Thus Fordell was restored with great pain and much love for the second time in its history. So the great fortress had become alive again, a great and glorious stone womb in which to collect and worship beautiful and amusing things, to give joy and delight to all who visit the ancient fortalice. Every man's home is his castle. For me my castle is my home but more it is the very expression of my soul within and without. And every year we extend and enlarge the idyllic nature of the house and garden for all to enjoy.[44]

Fairbairn's language is lyrical throughout, full of metaphor, glorifying the building and loosely describing it both as a 'great fortress' and an 'ancient fortalice'. It is reminiscent of the language used by Queen Marie of Romania, another wealthy owner with

a romantic disposition, about her restoration of Castle Bran (*See* Chapter 7). Fairbairn lived in Fordell until his death, although by then he had a second wife, Sam, living with him. In 1987, Fordell featured in *Living in Scotland*, a sumptuously illustrated coffee-table book about twenty-eight special homes. Fordell was described in only slightly less flowery language as a 'personal paradise and refuge':

> Some twenty years ago, Nicholas Fairbairn purchased a crumbling castle in Fife for the kind of sum which nowadays might buy a reasonable overcoat. [Nicholas Fairbairn's predecessor, a local businessman, had paid £100 for Fordell in 1952, when he bought it from Lord Attlee, Earl of Buckinghamshire.] Since then, love, dedication and physical effort have transformed this 14th century Clan Henderson keep into a personal paradise and a refuge from his often controversial political and legal life. An accomplished artist and admirer of beautiful things Fairbairn takes as much pride in his disciplined garden as in the interiors of Fordell Castle, which he has filled with eccentric acquisitions and personal memorabilia.[45]

It is clear, both from his writing and the passage above, that Fairbairn viewed his castle residence both as a reflection of his personal identity and as a bulwark against the outside world.

The 'Real' Professionals – the Architects

Fourteen castles were bought and restored by architects:

Hillslap — Philip Mercer
Pitcullo — Roy Spence
Ballone — Lachlan Stewart
Castle Leslie — David Leslie
Edinample, Peffermill and Liberton
  House — Nicholas Groves-Raines
Keith Hall, Cullen House and Formakin
  (early twentieth-century fake tower
  house built by Robert Lorimer)
  — Kit Martin
Kisimul — Robert Lister Macneil
Methven — Ken Murdoch
Gagie House — France Smoor
Old Sauchie — Sandy Leask

They, naturally, all acted as their own project managers. Lachlan Stewart of Ballone expressed the advantages and disadvantages: 'Because I am an architect, I know how to save money! I have done all the design work myself, and we have used local sawmills. The downside is that it has taken us five years to do what someone else could do in one.'

Keith Hall and Cullen are grand houses, which Kit Martin converted into large apartments. He bought speculatively in order to develop the properties and sell them on, while Nicholas Groves-Raines lived and worked in his properties before moving on to the next one. The other architects

Torwood Castle in 2011 (Courtesy of Richard Paxman)

all lived in their restored castles, at least for some time. As conservationists, those who worked in the 1960s and '70s were unusual members of their profession, at a time when Modernist ideas prevailed and architects were trained in designing new buildings rather than rescuing historic ones. Two of the architects also fall into the group of family heritage restorers – Robert Lister Macneil (Kisimul) and David Leslie (Leslie Castle).

In 1979, David Leslie, an architect for the City of Aberdeen, drove out to look again at Leslie Castle, where his father had taken him to visit as a boy so that they could view the original family seat. Almost on a whim, he ended up buying the ruin with a couple of acres of land for a small sum of money. The castle had been abandoned in the nineteenth century and had piles of rubble within its walls, some 8ft high. For ten years, he and his wife worked at the restoration of the castle, organising 'rubble rallies' with their friends to clear the stones and learning how to make stained and leaded glass for the windows. Eventually, they opened the castle as a small, private hotel and ran it for overseas business people until they sold up in 1998.

Ian Begg, the distinguished architect who supervised the restoration of many ruined towers and castles, eventually built his own twentieth-century castle called Ravenscraig, in Plockton.

The Entrepreneurs

The entrepreneurs planned from the start to make money from the buildings that they restored, either by selling them on, by building and developing property in the castle grounds or by running a business that capitalised on the castle's status and/or position. Ackergill, Broomhall, Borthwick, Comlongon, Glenapp, Fenton and Duncraig are all large castellated buildings that were turned into hotels or upmarket, catered accommodation by their new restoring owners. Mary McMurtrie's nursery garden and the Whartons' deer farm were set up in the grounds of Balbithan and Midmar respectively. New housing, or 'enabling development', was built in the grounds of Gogar and Sundrum castles and sold on by the builder owners, and Spedlins was sold on in a not quite finished state, but presumably at a profit.

Glenapp Castle is a huge Victorian baronial mansion in Ayrshire, designed by David Bryce. It had become derelict after a series of owners had neglected its upkeep in the second half of the twentieth century. In 1993, it was bought by a young couple, Fay and Graham Cowan. Fay was working as a hotel manager, and Graham was a country vet. In the autumn of that year, they were taken to see Glenapp Castle by Fay's parents, who ran a chain of hotels, and had seen the property advertised for sale:

On rounding the last corner, past a pair of magnificent monkey-puzzle trees we had our first glimpse of our future home, Glenapp Castle. It was a completely breathtaking sight – a forgotten place – a sleeping beauty, like the castle in the fairy tale that slept for a hundred years. The lawns were meadows and the paths merely suggested themselves by a dip in the ground. The windows were black and peeling and many were rotted completely away like missing teeth. The huge oak doors hung loose and creaking on their hinges. That day we stayed only a little while, but we were completely hooked. Nothing else would ever come close to this:

this first year was spent trying to get our plans passed by the local planning department, and making a start on the thirty acres of neglected garden and woodland. It took days for us even to get into the walled garden and the greenhouses alone were to take three months of joiner work and hundreds of panes of glass to restore. In the early days we had to switch four different hot water tanks on, to get scalding hot water in our bathroom. If we switched one off the water was instantly stone cold. Our bathroom was bigger than some of our friend's flats, and boasted a row of nine fitted wardrobes as well as for some reason, a bidet on wheels.

Like many castle purchases (Barholm included) negotiations with the owners were protracted, and, in this case, it took over a year before a leasehold was agreed and a further five years before they were able to buy it. Six years were spent on the restoration:

Our first year was spent 'camping' in the master bedroom, along with four electric fires, a four-poster bed with its own chandelier, and a geriatric Springer Spaniel. We were often asked if we weren't nervous of living alone in a vast deserted castle, but to us, Glenapp has never felt like anything other than a much loved home, despite its enormous size and we were just delighted to be here. Much of

They moved into the castle just in time to make their rescue more effective:

Fay and I moved into the castle in June 1994, ten days before the lease actually came into effect, mainly to try and prevent the ever increasing flow of unwanted visitors intent on removing the fixtures and fittings from the by now caretakerless castle. Just in time, as it turned out, because that very weekend there had been some kind of party in the gardens and fires had been lit, the lawns were strewn with beer bottles and cans, the castle had been broken into and worst of all the beautiful sundial in the terraced garden had been smashed to pieces.

Helen Bailey and Borthwick Castle

Borthwick is an enormous U-shaped castle in Midlothian, near Edinburgh, built in 1430. It was derelict when Helen Bailey took it over, in 1972, on a ninety-nine-year lease from the Earl of Borthwick (she eventually managed to buy it several years later, as a result of strenuous negotiations), after approaching him and persuading him to let her have the castle. 'I came, I saw and was conquered. Totally captivated by a building, but a very special one. A massive, magnificent castle standing like a sentinel over the lovely hamlet of Borthwick.' She invoked a kind of mystical predestination:

> As I walked around its perimeter walls and absorbed the unspoilt countryside in which it is set, it seemed to me that my presence at this spot and at this time was the fulfillment of a date with destiny. This feeling, already strong, was enhanced when my ears picked up a quiet, insistent, plaintive cry for help, intermingled with the murmuring of the gently flowing burn.

Helen Bailey's story is atypical in many ways – the castle is huge, the end use was as a hotel, and the restorer was a single woman. Helen did not own the castle for some considerable time due to a poorly managed agreement with the old owners. The risks that she took were gargantuan. In some ways, however, the story of Borthwick Castle's restoration does fit the 'norm'. The work began in 1973, at the start of the heritage movement and Helen Bailey was a new owner who came from a very ordinary background (her father had been a cabinetmaker and she attended the local state secondary school in Edinburgh), she carried out the restoration using her earnings rather than inherited wealth. Although she worked as a business consultant and had had a career in television, Bailey was not rich. Her lack of sufficient income led to serious financial difficulties, whereby she only narrowly avoided foreclosure.

Helen Bailey described her restoration of Borthwick Castle in her book, *My Love Affair with Borthwick Castle*. A bookseller might place the book in the 'inspirational literature' section, as it describes the overcoming of great odds through a series of risky adventures to a satisfyingly achieved end. Her story is about triumph over adversity written as a drama, with ghosts, evildoers, celebrity visitors, comedy and, finally, romance, when a paying guest at the castle (successfully) proposed marriage to her. This rather fey account is in stark contrast to the straight words of Gerry Loadsman, who bought Borthwick, already restored, from Helen Bailey in 1984: 'I never had any intention of living in the castle. I bought it to own it, like buying a Bentley, a lovely car.' Yet it seems clear that both were motivated to buy by the romantic appeal of owning a Scottish castle. Helen Bailey's initial, almost otherworldly approach to Borthwick was soon tempered, or even reversed, by the scale of practical and financial difficulties she faced:

I did not anticipate the sleepless nights, the heartaches and the agonies I had to endure while the castle was under siege from irate creditors during my struggles to escape bankruptcy, nor how deeply I was to be hurt by the open, sometimes vicious hostility of local public opinion. Not in a million years would I have believed that I would have to suffer the slings and arrows of Local Government officials who, it seemed, genuinely believed that the best way to protect the castle was to preside over its decline.

In Helen Bailey's restoration, no financial support was received or asked for, despite her narrow escape from bankruptcy. 'One thing I will not do is to apply for government aid or grants. I will either succeed on my own as a commercial enterprise, or fail in the attempt. I refuse utterly to go around with a begging bowl, nor do I have the soup kitchen mentality that has done so much damage to this country.'[46] This extreme ideological stance caused her great financial worry. Additionally, although she did not take on the labour of the restoration work herself, like other castle owners, Helen Bailey suffered physical privations while it was going on:

> For the next three weeks we lived in the Gate House in very cramped conditions. But at least we were warm and could cook our food on a small calor gas stove. The luxury of having a bath, however, came to an abrupt end when a neighbour, who shared the same spring well, cut off our supply. This was the first sign of the hostility that we were to encounter in the hamlet of Borthwick ... My pioneering spirit was severely strained particularly when I fell sick with a stomach complaint. Because the lavatory was out of use, there was nothing for it but to find a secluded bush behind the Gate House.

Among many serious difficulties and setbacks, she claimed that the most unpleasant of her recollections was the grief resulting from the hostility of neighbours.

CHAPTER 4

RESTORATIONS
1945–79

Castles in Danger

The Second World War had wreaked a terrible toll on historic buildings throughout Europe, although the UK emerged relatively unscathed, at least from enemy fire. However, many country houses and castles were lost through attrition. John Harris was a young, aspiring architectural historian who visited over 200 derelict, grand country houses in England between 1946 and 1961. He wrote a tragi-comic narrative of despair: 'In my nomadic travels I discovered a situation that had no parallel elsewhere in Europe: a country of deserted country houses, many in extremis, most in a surreal limbo awaiting their fate. They suffered from vandalism, smelt of decay and dry rot, exuded a sense of hopelessness.'[47] Had Harris journeyed through Scotland, he would have been faced with the same sad scenes. Like Evelyn Waugh's fictional stately home, Brideshead, most houses of any size in the UK had been requisitioned during the war and used to accommodate field hospitals, prisoner-of-war camps, billeted troops or storage facilities for precious documents. Among these were around forty Scottish castles, some of which did not survive the neglect and damage of wartime occupation. Tullichewan Castle, near Loch Lomond, was demolished in 1954 and Redcastle in the Black Isle was vacated and stripped in the 1950s, having been used by the army during the war; it is still in a perilous state and on the Buildings at Risk Register. At least seven of these war-occupied castles were later rescued and restored from a semi-ruinous or derelict state: Borthwick, Castle of Mey, Dollarbeg, Duncraig, Johnstone (in progress), Lochnaw and Merchiston.

By the end of the Second World War, Scotland was a poor country. Indeed, in economic terms, Scotland's star had been waning since the start of the twentieth century; in 1945, the legacy of war was evident in the daily lives of ordinary people. A quarter of the population was still living in one- or two-roomed housing and a third of families had to share a toilet. Life in Scotland was particularly hard for the poor, but some inhabitants of the 'big hoose' also suffered. Christian Miller's evocative biographical narrative of a child's harsh life in Monymusk Castle in the 1920s[48] could probably have been echoed in the lives of many of those living in castles and large houses in the 1950s. Catherine Maxwell-Stewart reported that her grandmother had lived alone at Traquair Castle throughout the Second World War with no electricity and limited heating, and, even in the twenty-first century, some owners continue to live in damp castles with little heating and few domestic comforts. Many country houses and castles were lost through attrition. Mary, Duchess of Buccleuch recalled:

> The army moved into Bowhill with not a thing put away. The officers' sitting room was where all the Van Dykes were. It was terribly badly

used; the army did terrible things to the house, all the proverbial things that troops are supposed to do – hacking down the banisters to make firewood, and throwing darts at the pictures. They couldn't have done more harm, and ended up by nearly burning it down twice.[49]

Bowhill recovered and it remains a glorious stately home today. Others, such as Balconie Castle in the Highlands, which fell into disrepair after having been an army billet during the Second World War, were not so fortunate. It was blown up, riddled with dry rot, in 1968. The SAVE Britain's Heritage book, *Lost Houses of Scotland*, estimated that 450 'houses of architectural pretension' had been lost between 1900 and 1980. Among these were around eighty castles and towers.

The 1950s

In the depressed and difficult period directly after the Second World War, very little building activity took place in Scottish castles. In the 1950s, only five castles were bought for restoration by individuals. These include:

Castle of Mey in Caithness —
   the most northerly castle in the
   British mainland, bought by the
   recently widowed Queen Mother
Stobhall in Perthshire — bought
   by the Duke of Perth from the
   Earl of Ancaster
House of Aldie in Kinross-shire —
   bought by Mr Hope Dickson
Kisimul on the Island of Barra in
   the Western Isles — bought by
   the Macneil Clan Chief, Robert
   Lister Macneil
Torwood Castle near Falkirk —
   bought by Gordon Millar,
   a former fighter pilot

The Queen Mother was one of the first individual owners to restore a ruined castle after the Second World War, and it is possible she even helped to set the trend in the same way that Queen Victoria stoked interest in Highland castles at the end of the nineteenth century. The often-repeated story of the Queen Mother's decision to rescue the castle may be apocryphal but it has a ring of truth. It is said that she first saw what was then Barrogill Castle in 1952, while mourning the death of her husband, King George VI. Falling for its ruined, isolated charm, and hearing it was to be abandoned, she declared, 'Never! It's part of Scotland's heritage. I'll save it.' On the BBC website, that area's MP, Viscount Thurso, expands on the story:

> 'She saw this building and, curious,
> she came down the drive and found
> it with the family in one room and,
> I think, the sheep in the other room,'
> he said. 'She fell in love with it. It is
> the most beautiful, pretty small
> castle, very typical of what we had
> around Caithness in days gone by.

She determined to rescue it, which she did.' The castle was in need of major repair work after 120mph gales had lifted its lead roof and rolled it up 'like a can'.

The Queen Mother regularly travelled north to supervise the work, eventually moving in for holiday periods and restoring the ancient name of the sixteenth-century tower, the Castle of Mey. She was also heavily involved in the restoration of the castle gardens. The castle and gardens were private until after the Queen Mother's death in 2002, but are now open to the public for most of each summer.

Aldie Castle (also known as the House of Aldie), formerly a Mercer-Nairne house, was bought in 1952 by Archibald Hope Dickson, when he came to Scotland after working in the Far East. It had been reported as 'becoming ruinous' by the RCAHMS inspector in 1929. Hope Dickson employed the distinguished Edinburgh architect, Ian Lindsay, to draw up plans for the restoration as a gentleman's residence and furnished the house with works of art.

Not all castle restoration plans were successful. Gordon Millar was the first of the 'hobby restorers', who purchased a ruin cheaply with a view to managing a DIY restoration. Millar, a chartered

Pitcullo Castle

accountant and former Second World War pilot, certainly had a vision of restoring Torwood Castle, but no means with which to do so. He bought the castle from the Carron Ironworks Company in 1957 and moved in to the ruined shell, living there without electricity or running water for many years, but he never came near to finishing any work that might count as a restoration. Torwood is now owned by the Torwood Trust and is still a ruin.

The 1960s

The 1960s saw the beginnings of a general rise in affluence across Britain, with more social housing, rising wages, greater leisure time for workers and the expansion of the middle classes. In Scotland, it became easier to get around, as a programme of road and bridge building, coupled with more reliable and more affordable cars, allowed people to visit remote historic properties (increasing numbers of which were open to the public) and perhaps to dream of owning one. The pace of restorations now began to hot up, despite the continuation of hard-nosed attitudes towards old buildings. Pressure was beginning to build in favour of protecting the built heritage, but progress towards a climate of conservation was still slow; more than twice as many castles were destroyed as were restored during the 1960s. Ten castles were purchased for restoration. Balfluig, Balbithan, Breachacha, Castle Stalker, Fordell, Garth, Kinkell, Towie Barclay, Inverquharity and Pitcullo were all bought by new owners bent on acquiring a castle to restore and live in (or, in the case of Garth, to be used as a holiday home).

Pitcullo was restored in the late 1960s by Mr and Mrs Roy Spence. It was restored for a second time by Sir Angus Grossart, merchant banker, in the late 1970s after a serious fire.

Towie Barclay in Aberdeenshire was bought in 1969 from the Aberdeen Endowments Trust and restored over a period of seven years by the musician Marc Ellington, now a passionate conservationist and executive director of the Scottish Traditional Skills Training Centre, a charity that provides training courses on conservation. Towie Barclay won a Saltire Award for its restoration. Marc Ellington very much approves of the DIY 'hands-on' approach taken by so many of the restorers whose work:

Kinkell before it was restored
(© Richard Paxman)

... has been almost entirely controlled and directed by the owners themselves using their architects and professional advisers principally for the purpose of providing working drawings and communicating with relevant public authorities. This degree of personal involvement and commitment by owners has contributed greatly to their restorations' success and individuality.[50]

Kinkell is a sixteenth-century tower in Inverness-shire, which had been expanded in the eighteenth century and was ruinous and in danger of collapse when Gerald Laing and his wife purchased it from a farmer in 1964. Laing's full-length book tells the story of the reconstruction of a Scottish castle (the subtitle of his book), but with many discursive asides about art, history, politics and social issues. Laing's restoration of Kinkell was a dream fulfilment, as described by *Scots Magazine*:

As a solitary and alienated child growing up in the unlovely environs of post-war industrial Newcastle, Gerald Laing found the perfect antidote to his loneliness lay in the fantasy world he created by literally disappearing into the past. Peddling his bicycle deep into the so-called Debatable Lands along the Anglo-Scottish border, he found a landscape littered with picturesque peel towers and the remains of ancient castles. The ruins had an almost hypnotic hold over him, so much so that he was determined to possess a castle of his own and, at the age of 14, even went so far as to enquire the price of the peel tower at Corbridge. He could see exactly how the ruined tower could be restored. It was a vision he was to nurture for 20 years.[51]

Laing made a gung-ho start to his restoration as soon as had made the purchase of the tower:

Balfluig Castle

Bright and early next morning we arrived at Kinkell, unlocked our tool shed and began work, innocents abroad in the building trade. We parked the wheelbarrow directly under one of the windows of the Great Hall, took our pick and shovel upstairs and started loosening the pile of plaster and rubbish on the floor.[52]

Despite the picture painted above, Laing's approach to Kinkell was thoughtful, intellectual and artistic, with a moral underpinning. Intellectually, 'The point of rebuilding Kinkell Castle was to savour the facts of sixteenth century architecture, and by doing so to understand more of the past and its similarities, rather than its differences from the present.'[53] As a sculptor, he saw Kinkell as essentially a giant sculpture and approached it as such. But, unlike the many owners who put much effort into sourcing 'authentic' materials, Laing took a firm position against the acquisition of fittings that were already old, or made to appear old:

What you think you'll get and what you actually end up with are two entirely different things. I found that when we were halfway through building a new castle. Morally we could do nothing else. I had already decided that the only way to repair and replace parts of the structure was to use similar materials in a workmanlike way. To use old beams, or, worse, to disfigure and stain them artificially would be a hypocrisy based on romanticism.

It would be an affectation even to trim them with an adze.

Despite his desire to be 'honest' and to work with the building sympathetically, Laing reported using cement and concrete liberally in his rebuilding, which would be viewed as conservation vandalism in the twenty-first century. He did, however, take a seriously aesthetic view of the interior design. When talking of internal plastering:

I experimented with various alternatives; first leaving the large stones in the wall uncovered and following the outer edges of the long and short corner stones around the various openings – doorways, windows, gun loops and arrow slits. This succeeded in making the room look like the Medieval Bar of a Chicago hotel and was a total failure.[54]

In the preface to the second edition, Laing explained why he decided to pull down an eighteenth-century wing:

I appreciate fully the reason why the extension was added in the eighteenth century. I certainly could use the extra space and convenience which it provided. But I do not regret having demolished it; I do not regret the desire for the pure and original architectural expression which inspired the reconstruction of this castle, for that, I believe, is the element which excites the interest of so many people.

The Murdochs also took down an extension at Methven, although the reason there seemed to be pragmatic rather than aesthetic, and at Cramond the Jamiesons added an extension later (where there was evidence of a former building), as did the owner of Couston Castle when it was restored. Although in the twenty-first century it is exceedingly difficult to get planning permission for either demolitions or additions, in the 1960s, '70s and '80s a number of castle restorers were able to make significant changes to their buildings and also to take a degree of control over the work that would be unlikely to be permitted now in a Grade A listed building. Laing justified his tight personal control in terms of the difficulty of visualising the future:

> This is a problem architects have to face the whole time; once the plan is delineated they are committed to its original form by cost. They cannot easily alter course whatever magic island or intriguing inlet reveals itself on the voyage. I had made many changes of plan during the rebuilding of Kinkell which, even though some were major ones, were achieved simply and comparatively inexpensively, largely because I was using direct labour and had total control myself. If I had used a contractor, not only would the basic costs have been trebled before we began, but also any alteration of the original plan would have been difficult to implement and financially prohibitive.[55]

Laing's restoration from a roofless ruin to a furnished home took, astonishingly, less than one year. The book was an inspiration for Lord David Steel, restorer of Aikwood, whose wife, Judy, gave him a copy, knowing that he was interested in restoring a castle or tower. Tom Clarke, owner of Kilmartin and Lochhouse castles, also credited Kinkell and Laing's 'inspirational book' for his interest in restoring ruins. We, too, were given a copy at the start of our restoration project, by Peter Kormylo of Abbot's Tower, and I was thrilled and fascinated by Laing's story.

Inverquharity was bought by Sandy Grant, a former colonial civil servant. Garth Castle in Glenlyon was restored by a Mr Fry, who had bought Garth to use as a holiday home:

> Designed initially by a local firm in Aberfeldy, Mr. Fry's work was not at all archaeologically based and would not receive listed building consent now. What had been built of Heiton's caphouse was cleared off to form a sun-deck rook and the upper floors treated as one large space with a sleeping gallery, the English architect Leonard Manasseh being brought in too late to achieve a more presentable result ... Although Garth itself was a failure, at least in historical and architectural terms, the concept caught on.[56]

Balfluig in Aberdeenshire was bought and restored by Mark Tennant, barrister son of Sir Iain Tennant, in 1966–7.

Midmar Castle

Balbithan, also in Aberdeenshire, was purchased by the widowed artist Mary McMurtrie. She had bought the castle, which originally dates from 1600, in 1960 and painstakingly restored it to its former glory. She transformed its gardens into a leading north east nursery, specialising in rock plants, alpines and traditional garden flowers. She was to run the nursery until she was in her 80s, when she finally retired to live on the outskirts of Aberdeen, carrying on her other career as a renowned botanical artist, almost until her death at the age of 101, in 2003.

So, in the 1960s can be seen the beginnings of the concept of castle restoration as a viable pursuit for new owners, but still on a small scale, and mainly in the hands of relatively well-off professional owners: two artists, one musician, one barrister, an architect, an army commissioned officer and a man who could afford to have a castle restored as his holiday home (Mr Fry, about whom nothing else is known). All of the restorations were carried out quite quickly, except for Breachacha, which became a long-term project. The castle restoration movement as an adventurous pursuit for young couples of limited means was yet to take off. And that would depend upon a change of climate in which the built heritage was valued instead of being generally derided.

The Heritage Industry

The 1970s – Horrors and Hope

In 1972, John Cornforth had been commissioned by the Historic Houses Committee of the British Tourist Authority to write an independent report on the future of country houses in Britain. He concluded gloomily that the outlook was worse than in 1945: 'then at least there was the hope that things might get better, as indeed they did; but now there seems only the certainty that they will get worse.'[57] Happily, he was wrong. The turning point in attitude came in 1974, when Marcus Binney and John Harris organised 'The Destruction of the Country House' exhibition at the Victoria & Albert Museum in London for the new curator, Roy Strong.

The exhibition's 'Hall of Destruction' was a fantasy of tumbling columns illustrating some of the 1,000 or so country houses demolished over the preceding century.

> The impact on the public was overwhelming, for they alighted upon it turning a corner, having been wafted along by an opening section on country house glories. And then they came face to face with this. Many was the time I stood in that exhibition watching the tears stream down the visitors' faces as they battled to come to terms with all that had gone.[58]

The V&A website states: 'Such was the concern generated by the exhibition that from 1975 demolition of historic country houses came to a virtual halt.' This perhaps rather overstates the case, but the tide was indeed turning fast, not only in Britain, but also throughout Europe. The year 1975 was European Architectural Heritage Year, during which the European Charter of the Architectural Heritage was adopted by the Council of Europe. The principles laid out the explicit and uncompromising message that the European heritage of historical buildings was in danger and efforts must be made to save it. The justification being the social value of historical awareness: 'This heritage should be passed on to future generations in its authentic state and in all its variety as an essential part of the memory of the human race. Otherwise, part of man's awareness of his own continuity will be destroyed.'[59]

In Scotland, another significant event at this time was when the 12th Duke of Argyll organised the swift rebuilding of Inverary Castle after the very serious fire on 5 November 1975, which, according to the historian Ian Gow, 'reflected a turning point in attitudes to preservation, and inspired the conservation of further houses.'[60]

The 1970s saw a dramatic fall in the numbers of demolitions at the same time as a great surge in restorations. Despite the upturn in the number of castles restored in the 1970s, however, it was not an easy time to be involved in a major building project. There was rapid inflation in building prices – more than 25 per cent in 1977 – and, by 1979, the mortgage interest rate was 15 per cent and still rising. Nevertheless, increasing numbers were becoming engaged in the castle restoration adventure.

The 1970s – Castles Restored

Nigel Tranter campaigned for years to save many Scottish towers, or 'fortalices', and was instrumental in finding new restoring owners for several, including Ballencrieff and Harthill:

> They are very much a wasting, though irreplaceable, asset. Although we are the envy of so many from lands less favoured in this respect, all too few of our own people either know, appreciate or care for them. Especially, unhappily, local authorities, into whose hands many of them fall. [61]

He was particularly alarmed by 'a craze for demolition among certain of our local government authorities, which seem to prefer anything modern, however unattractive and poorly built, to anything ancient.'[62] It is not fanciful to compare the deliberate destruction of architecturally significant buildings that symbolised unwanted ideologies to book burnings – an attempt, usually futile, but powered by rage and fear, to purge despised objects. Similar emotional reactions of distress and a deep sense of sadness are aroused by the violent destruction of both books and buildings, as both represent aspects of culture and civilisation whose loss is a break with the past and leaves the future bleak. Books can usually be reprinted, however, but a destroyed building is unlikely ever to be rebuilt.

The story of the fight – ultimately successful – by conservationists to save Rossend Castle in Burntisland, Fife, whose Labour Council decided that its ancient castle should be destroyed as a symbol of former feudal oppression, exemplifies the struggles that went on in many places to save condemned historic buildings. It is a tale full of drama and, from a twenty-first century perspective, shocking. John Gifford described it as 'the material for a conservationist's fairy story (despised frog kissed by beautiful maiden and transformed into a handsome if heavy-featured prince)'.[63] The architects firm of Robert Hurd & Partners, after a long battle, eventually managed to purchase the sixteenth-century castle from the local council for £350, in order to restore it and turn it into offices for the practice – but only after the demolition crew had already moved their equipment onto the site. Harry Gourlay, MP for Kirkcaldy Burghs, wanted to 'erect a palisade around the castle high enough and strong enough to keep children out and also to prevent people from seeing the monster, remove all mechanical implements which are sustaining the building at the moment and allow it to fall into a state of utter decay'. He attacked the Secretary of State for agreeing to save the building from demolition and said he would raise the matter in the Commons. He went on; 'as far as I can see there is absolutely no argument for preserving this building. It does not even look like a castle and has no beauty at all in my eyes'. Another local politician was equally against saving Rossend Castle. Dean of Guild Bolam, amazed to read of the historical interest, said, 'I would like to know what comprises historical. I understand that Mary Queen of Scots stayed there one night – that's nothing to get hysterical about, never mind historical.'

It is interesting to note that the 'look' of the building was an important factor in influencing opinion against its retention. Appearance is highly significant in shaping perceptions of whether or not a castle 'deserves' the appellation; the name itself is not always sufficient. Buittle Tower in Galloway had its turrets removed in the nineteenth century, when it was let out to a tenant farmer; these symbols of lordly status were considered too grand for the new, lowly inhabitants of the building. As the conservation campaigner, Moultrie Kelsall, put it in 1961: 'To Scotsmen-on-the-make the fact that a building was traditional in design, and of a respectable age, were twin reasons why it should be destroyed.'[64]

In the 1970s, Blackhall Manor in Paisley, which had been bequeathed to the town, was eventually so neglected, vandalised and dangerous that there were calls for it to be demolished.

But Paisley Council took a different view
to the council at Burntisland. In 1978,
the council considered the demolition
option but the public outcry was such
that the order was given to shore up
the building and brick up the windows
against further damage. In 1982, Alex
Strachan acquired the property and set
about the gargantuan task of restoring it.
It may be that the very public rescue of
Rossend had a second beneficial effect,
in the saving of Blackhall Manor. So,
although in the Scotland of the 1950s,
'60s and '70s, castle ruins continued

Balgonie Castle

to crumble, at risk from 'the improver, the moderniser, the demolisher and the vandal'[65] by the mid-1970s, fortunately, the tide began to turn in favour of the conservationists and restorers. The reasons why these changes in attitude and behaviour came about are to be found in a complex mix of economic circumstances, social class changes and media involvement, coupled with the interventions of a number of very determined individual campaigners and architects.

The pattern of castle ownership had also begun to change quite markedly by the 1970s. Seventeen castle restoration projects were begun by new owners who had purchased the building with the express purpose of restoration. These were:

Aiket	Gilknockie
Allardice	Harthill
Balgonie	Midmar
Balmuto	Niddry
Barscobe	Pitfichie
Blackhall	Powrie
Cramond	Ravenstone
Edinample	Rusco
Fa'side	

Several of these were bought by do-it-yourself restorers, in the same mould as Gerald Laing at Kinkell. In addition, Maxwelton House (home of Annie Laurie of the song), although not

ruinous or derelict, won a Saltire Award in 1973 and a Civic Trust Architectural Heritage Award in 1975 for major restoration and reconstruction work by Michael Laird, commissioned by Mr and Mrs Stenhouse. Castle Stuart was leased, rather than bought, by the Canadian couple, Charles and Elizabeth Stuart, from the Earl of Moray. They reported spending $2 million on the restoration of the castle between 1977 and 2010, partly financed by paying guests. The Stuarts live in a cottage in the grounds and run the castle as a private hotel.

The social spread of the 1970s restorers was much wider than previously. Two Americans were among the 1970s restorers – Harry Boswell, a lawyer and property developer, who restored Balmuto Tower, a Boswell castle in Fife, and Ann Tweedy Savage, a writer, traveller and philanthropist who restored Harthill Castle in Aberdeenshire, after taking advice from Nigel Tranter. Barscobe Castle was restored by Sir Hugh Wontner, managing director of the Savoy hotel group and Lord Mayor of London; he had purchased the large estate on which it stood in 1961, having rented Barscobe House, also on the estate, as a holiday home in previous years. Dame Bridget D'Oyly Carte, head of the D'Oyly Carte opera company, advised him on the project and she became the first tenant once the restoration was finished, living there until her death in 1985. Barscobe Castle is still owned by Sir Hugh Wontner's descendants.

Midmar Castle is one of the five grand castles of Aberdeenshire built by the Bell family of masons. The other four – Crathes, Fraser, Drum and Craigievar – are now owned by the National Trust. All are chateau-like in their airy grandeur; it is not surprising that Midmar, with ten bedrooms and 185 acres, had a price tag of £5 million when it went on the market in 2009, although it never realised this sum. Midmar had been empty since 1842 when it was restored, in 1977, by Ric Wharton, an entrepreneur from the shipping and oil industries, who used the value of the house to underwrite a risky, but ultimately successful, expedition in 1981 to recover £50 million in Russian gold, which had gone down with HMS *Edinburgh* in the Second World War. The Whartons ran a deer farm in the grounds of Midmar Castle for several years, selling bloodstock on the international market.

Pitfichie was restored by an Aberdeen antiques dealer, Colin Wood, Edinample by the architect Nicholas Groves-Raines and Powrie by a BBC journalist, Gillian Strickland, and her politician husband, Peter Clarke. Having won Powrie Castle in a competition run by the National Trust for Scotland in the mid-1970s, she and her husband lived in a caravan for part of the time that the restoration work was being carried out. Three owners who purchased ruined castles in the 1970s did not complete the restoration of their castle (Balgonie, Niddry and Ravenstone), and sold them on to other would-be restorers. None of these

Balgonie Castle chapel, decorated for a wedding

Inverary Castle (© Stara Blazkova)

three properties was fully finished at the time of writing, but all three were lived in and still being worked on by their new owners.

The current Laird of Balgonie is Raymond Morris, who lives in the castle with his family. They have been continuing to rebuild, restore and maintain this large and complex building, whose tower dates to the fourteenth century, with the help of volunteers and with limited resources, over the past forty years. There is still a huge amount to do, including replacing the leaking tower roof. The Balgonie family's main source of income is from weddings, conducted by candlelight in the castle's own chapel, with receptions held in the Great Hall.

Aiket Castle

For fifteen years, in the 1960s and early 1970s, Robert and Katrina Clow visited nearly every tower house in the central belt of Scotland, armed with copies of Nigel Tranter's, *The Fortified House in Scotland*, and MacGibbon and Ross', *The Castellated and Domestic* *Architecture of Scotland*. They were searching for a suitable tower or castle to restore and live in. Finally, in 1976, they purchased Aiket Castle in Ayrshire for £6,000; 'two intact vaults and traces of a fifteenth century stairway on the ground floor, a generous stair to the first floor; three walls on the first and (what had been) the second floors; the open sky above.' Until the 1950s, it had been inhabited, latterly by cattle on the ground floor, two families on the first floor (without running water or electricity) and chickens in the attic. Then, in 1957, it was burned out and the building fell further and further into a dangerously ruinous state.

The Clows decided, having researched the history of Aiket and examined the building in great detail, to take it back to the fifteenth- and sixteenth-century core, although this was against the advice of the Historic Buildings Council inspector at the time. Aiket had been rebuilt at least three times – in the sixteenth, seventeenth and eighteenth centuries. It was now a shell and needed coherence in its structure. Robert and Katrina reinstated doors, fireplaces and turrets in a sympathetic revival of the earliest part of the tower, carrying out much of the heavy work themselves, on a tight budget and at a time of 27 per cent inflation. They won a Europa Nostra Award for their restoration, vindicating their decision to restore the original building. Aiket was one of the first restored castles we visited after buying Barholm, and we were grateful for the Clows' welcome and their advice. Robert told us to make sure that we used hardwood for the window frames, to avoid replacing them every few years; on his advice we changed our building specification, paid extra for oak and remain glad that we did. The one softwood door at Barholm, leading on to the wall

walk, has started to rot away already, only seven years after it was installed.

Cramond Tower is a small sixteenth-century building that was almost certainly originally part of a larger complex and was part of a residence of the Bishops of Dunkeld. It sits on the outskirts of Edinburgh. In 1889, MacGibbon and Ross lamented that the tower was 'in an unfortunate condition, being entirely crowned with ivy, which has got such a hold of it (the branches in some places going through the walls) as to greatly imperil its safety'. Nothing was done, however, until the 1960s, when Edinburgh Town Council removed most of the vegetation and crowned the barrel roof with a concrete cap. On discovering later that they did not actually own the building, further restoration was abandoned and it was again left to deteriorate until Eric Jamieson and his son, George, bought it in 1978:

> It seemed a pity that such a unique building should be allowed to succumb to the twin ravages of time and vandalism, and I began to make enquiries regarding its ownership with a view to acquiring and restoring it … As an amateur antiquarian my original intention, when I bought the tower in 1978, had been to manage the project as a hobby, with no particular time-scale, but then my eldest son saw the restored tower as a place in which he could live and carry on his work as a wildlife artist and a taxidermist, and he inspired a new degree of urgency for the task. [66]

Not that it was quick. Nearly two years were spent on acquiring the building from the previous owners, the legatees of the late Mrs Craigie-Halkett, and obtaining the necessary permissions. This was followed by a further four years of part-time work before residence was possible. The architect was Ian Begg. There were difficulties during the building work, as well as before, and the usual stories of risk and physical hardship: 'Vandalism was rife, during the early phases, and to avoid the use of unattended scaffolding – an invitation to daring hooligans – my son carried out much of the external pointing and the laying of 5,000 old Scots slates from the safety of his mountaineering harness.'[67]

Jamieson's account emphasises the perseverance needed to complete a castle restoration project, and the vast amount of paperwork it generates. Staying power in the face of obstacles was an essential attribute. However, he enjoyed the DIY project, and took pride in it, despite the difficulties:

It would not be true, however, to imply that the work was wholly laborious. There were days of brilliant sunshine when everyone just sat around on the flat roof, level with the surrounding treetops, and admired the magnificent panorama of the city to the south of the Firth of Forth to the north. There were other days when the tea break would be in front of a roaring fire in the main hall, and there were unique rewards, such as the occasion when a visitor slapped his hand on a completely re-built stone wall and remarked, 'They don't build walls like that nowadays!'[68]

In many ways, the 1970s was a time of glorious excitement, with almost a frontier spirit among would-be castle restorers. Things were gradually about to change, however.

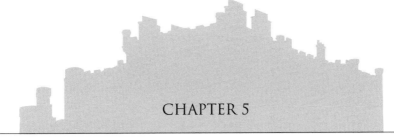

CHAPTER 5

RESTORATIONS
SINCE 1980

The 1980s – Politics and Passion

Heritage conservation had had a promising decade in the 1970s, with growing concern for the care of historic buildings. The 1980s were dominated by the politics of Margaret Thatcher. Although she was not personally much interested in heritage, many of her party members belonged to the landowning classes; thus, it was politically expedient for the Conservatives in government to be seen to be helpful to the conservation lobby. Patrick Cormack, historian, Conservative Member of Parliament and founder secretary of the parliamentary All Party Committee for the Heritage, had written *Heritage in Danger* in 1978, in which he invoked lyrical images of the English country house, using emotive language that was typical of the impassioned heritage rhetoric of the time:

These houses are a special public possession for it is in them and in our churches that we perhaps come closest to the soul and spirit of England ... They are a unique and gentle blend of the craftsman's art and rural beauty, filled with the familiar acquisitions of generations: the collections of the dilettanti; the library of the local scholar-statesman; the domestic accumulations which themselves give a living commentary on men and manners through the centuries. Set in their spacious parklands and often containing priceless collections, our country houses are part of the very fabric of our civilization.[69]

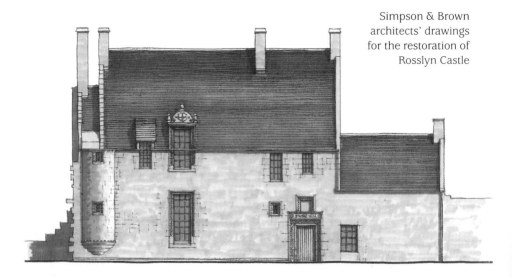

Simpson & Brown architects' drawings for the restoration of Rosslyn Castle

Although Cormack was talking specifically of England, Inverary Castle, restored by the Duke of Argyll after a fire in 1975, is a magnificent eighteenth-century castellated mansion, of the type to which Cormack was doubtless referring when he wrote of the 'very fabric of our civilization'.

The arguments of the English conservation lobby percolated to Scotland and helped the cause of Scottish castles. But Cormack's sentimental, Arcadian view of the English past was condemned by the American author, Martin Wiener, whose robustly pro-capitalist and anti-conservationist views were much admired by the New Right of the Thatcher government. One story – possibly apocryphal – is that Keith Joseph, Secretary of State for Education and Science, had handed a copy of Wiener's book, *English Culture and the Decline of the Industrial Spirit 1850–1980*, to all Cabinet members. From the mid-1980s, a reaction to the rise of heritage set in. Heritage was seen as having been appropriated by conservatism and the political forces of the Right, despite the New Right's rejection of sentimental views of the past, and came to represent, for some academics at least, pejorative and almost comic connotations. Thus, the built heritage was at risk from forces on both sides of the political spectrum – a dangerous position to be in.

In 1979, Patrick Wright returned to Britain from a five-year stay in North America and reported, 'I felt as if I had inadvertently stumbled into some sort of anthropological museum.' [70] He wrote an excoriating review of a country in decline because of its emphasis on heritage, *On Living in an Old Country*, published in 1985, which was followed, in 1987, by the publication of Robert Hewison's *The Heritage Industry*.[71] Hewison claimed that culture in the UK was being stifled by an emphasis on the past. Both books had a profound influence on academic political and social science, with their argument that heritage and 'Victorian values' were being cynically manipulated by the Thatcher government for political gain. In the mid-1980s, the anti-conservation lobby held sway among the elite majority of academics and architects – but they made a powerful royal enemy.

Prince Charles stepped into the heritage and conservation debate in 1984. The occasion was the 150th anniversary of the Royal Institute of British Architects, the setting Hampton Court Palace. Charles had been invited to present the Royal Gold Medal for Architecture, but instead of uttering a few platitudes, as had been expected, he launched an outspoken attack on architecture in post-war Britain:

> At last, after witnessing the wholesale destruction of Georgian and Victorian housing in most of our cities, people have begun to realise that it is possible to restore old buildings and, what is more, that there are architects willing to undertake such projects. For far too long, it seems to me, some planners and architects have consistently ignored the feelings and wishes of the mass of ordinary people in this country.[72]

Charles' criticism of modernist architecture and his points about conservation and lack of consultation struck an immediate chord with the public and the media, although he was held up to ridicule by the architectural community for his supposed lack of knowledge and understanding. But Prince Charles was generally lauded by the popular press and went on to make a documentary film about architecture with the BBC, *A Vision of Britain*, in 1988. In 1989, an accompanying book was published, in which he pointed the finger of blame for the destruction of the built heritage firmly at the architectural profession:

The further I delve into the shadowy world of architecture, planning and property development the more I become aware of various interest groups … I believe it was the architectural establishment, or a powerful group within it, which made the running in the 50s and 60s. It was they who set the cultural agenda.[73]

Prince Charles' grandmother, the Queen Mother, had been one of the early post-war castle restorers and he was defending a cause close to his heart. His analysis was correct: the cultural agenda was indeed set against conservation in the 1950s and '60s and the architectural establishment was, at least partly, to blame.

1980s Castles Restored

Despite the ideological debates raging among the great and the good, castle restoration flourished in Scotland. Seventeen castles were purchased for restoration by individuals in the 1980s, mostly for rebuilding as a home or holiday home. They were:

Ackergill	Hillslap
Castle Grant	Law
Castle Levan	Leslie
Comlongon	Mains
Couston	Peffermill House
Craigcaffie	Spedlins
Forter	Tillycairn
Gagie House	Terpersie
Hatton	

All of these restorers were 'new' owners who had not had any connection with the buildings previously and were not from the landowning classes. The eighteen new owners also represented a wide range of backgrounds and professions.

In addition, Dundee District Council restored Dudhope Castle, despite earlier moves by the council to demolish it in 1958. It is now used as a conference centre and office accommodation, surrounded by a municipal park. Two 'old' families had their towers restored in the 1980s: Muckrach Castle, near Aviemore, was restored after an Inverness planning officer had called upon the

Gough-Calthorpe family to meet their obligations to look after the fine but terribly ruinous tower that stood on their land. The conservation architect, Ian Begg, was employed to carry out the restoration and described Muckrach as ruinous and frail, but with 'enormous presence' and 'a real little gem to work on'. He admired it so much that he has modelled his own contemporary tower home, in Plockton, on Muckrach. The castle is now available for rent as a four-bedroom holiday let. Whytbank Tower in the Borders, which had been very ruinous, was restored by the Pringle family, who were the original builders in the sixteenth century.

Rosslyn Castle, situated near to the world famous Rosslyn Chapel, on a dramatic cliff above the River Esk, was restored by Simpson & Brown, architects for the Landmark Trust, as holiday accommodation, although it is still owned by the Earl of Rosslyn. One can only imagine that Dan Brown's book, *The Da Vinci Code*, must have had a very positive effect on bookings, since visitors to the chapel increased by over 50 per cent after its publication and it is now one of the most popular tourist attractions in Scotland.

Also restored by the Landmark Trust for holiday accommodation was the tall and rather gaunt Castle of Park, in Wigtownshire. Built by Thomas Hay in the 1590s, it had been abandoned in the 1830s and was occupied by farmworkers for a time until it became completely derelict in the 1950s, when its eighteenth-century wings were removed by the Ministry of Works. In the 1970s, it was taken over by Historic Scotland and a programme of restoration begun. It was finally made habitable by the Landmark Trust, who installed heating, lighting, bathrooms and a kitchen, in the early 1990s.

In this decade there were several 'serial restorers' and also architects. Spedlins was restored by Stephen Yorke, who, according to Nick Gray, the present owner, restored houses to sell. The Grays, who have since made a lovely Renaissance garden beside the house, found that there was quite a bit to do when they initially bought the tower. The roof leaked. The septic tank did not work. There was no central heating and the open fire in the living room smoked to such an extent that it could not be used. However, having made the tower more comfortable and watertight, and having used Spedlins as a part-time home for some years, the Grays now live there permanently.

Two restorers had to give up their castles before completion. Hatton Castle was restored by Roderick Oliphant, who planned to make it a clan centre, but ran out of money just before it was finished; the building was repossessed and the restoration was later finished by the Anderson family. Law Castle was bought by a businessman, Mr Philips; the restoration was started but not finished and the building was sold. In this situation, the grant given for the restoration must be recovered:

Castle of Park, Wigtownshire

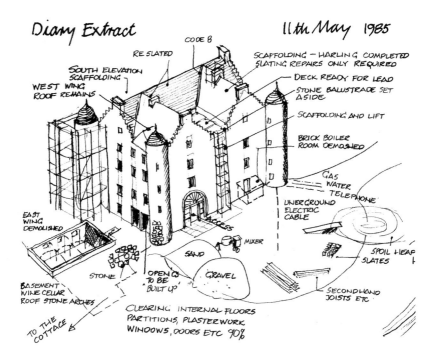

Diary Extract   **11th May 1985**

CODE B

RE SLATED

SOUTH ELEVATION SCAFFOLDING

WEST WING ROOF REMAINS

SCAFFOLDING — HARLING COMPLETED SLATING REPAIRS ONLY REQUIRED

DECK READY FOR LEAD

STONE BALUSTRADE SET ASIDE

SCAFFOLDING AND LIFT

BRICK BOILER ROOM DEMOSHED

GAS
WATER
TELEPHONE
UNDERGROUND ELECTRIC CABLE

EAST WING DEMOLISHED

MIXER

SPOIL HEAP SLATES

STONE

SAND

GRAVEL

OPENGS TO BE 'BUILT UP'

BASEMENT WINE CELLAR ROOF STONE ARCHES

SECONDHAND JOISTS ETC

TO THE COTTAGE

CLEARING INTERNAL FLOORS PARTITIONS, PLASTERWORK WINDOWS, DOORS ETC 90%

ACCESS

Ken Murdoch's diary on the restoration of Methven Castle

A spokesman for Historic Scotland said it was the organisation's statutory duty to try to recover the funds, adding that it was the £116,000 grant for the final phase of work that it was seeking to retrieve. 'If someone buys a historic property and receives a grant to aid the restoration of it but fails to comply with the conditions of the award, then it is our duty to recover it. Similarly, if someone sells a property that we had awarded grants to for a huge profit then we would also seek to recover a proportion of the profits. We can confirm that we are taking action to recover a proportion of the grant from the sale of Law Castle as part of our statutory requirements.'[74]

This was quite an unusual event in the history of restorations; Historic Scotland does not often take legal action against owners.

Couston was also restored by a businessman, Alastair Harper, who was obviously more successful financially than the owner of Law Castle. Ackergill Castle, sited on the edge of the wild Caithness coast, was derelict rather than ruinous when it was bought at auction from the Duff Dunbar family in 1986 and restored by a businessman, John Banister, and his partners, who turned it into luxury catered accommodation. The castle had been virtually uninhabited in recent years and was in danger of losing its roof, while its interior had hardly been touched since the 1920s. Music was still on the piano and a glass on the table when John Banister viewed it. The restoration and renovation of the castle, which was supported by Historic Scotland, cost around £400,000 for the building work, and a similar sum for decoration and furnishings.

An advertising executive and art collector, David Pearson, restored Castle Levan, where he and his wife lived until their retirement in 1995. Its current owners run it as a bed and breakfast establishment. Forter Castle in Perthshire was restored by Robert Pooley, owner of Pooley Aviation Ltd. Castle Grant was bought and re-roofed by Paul Dobson, then sold on before the restoration was finished. It was sold again a further six times between 1985 and 2006, its latest owner being the controversial Rangers Football Club chief, Craig Whyte. Craigcaffie in Galloway, a diminutive doll's house of a castle that was originally owned by the Earl of Stair, was restored by the Walkers, who engaged a firm of local architects to manage the restoration. It has been sold on and is now used by its owners as a holiday home. Mains Castle in East Kilbride was restored by the entertainer 'Big Rory' Mike Rowan and tiny Terpersie in Aberdeenshire was restored by an army officer, Captain Lachlan Rhodes. It, too, has been sold on and is used as a holiday home.

Methven Castle

Methven Castle is a large seventeenth-century castellated villa that was derelict and deteriorating when the architect, Ken Murdoch, and his wife, Anna, purchased it for restoration from a farmer in 1983. The west wing had been demolished in 1953, and, in 1984, the Murdochs demolished the east wing before commencing restoration work. The restoration of Methven Castle was a DIY project that Ken Murdoch described in a self-published book, beautifully illustrated with his own watercolour sketches, for which Professor Charles McKean wrote an introduction:

> This is the story of how a small family with limited resources took on an enormous historic monument in dire condition – and had

to take on the authorities as well. Yet the narrative, accompanied by enormously valuable, quirky and often very funny diary sheets, is so modest that we have to imagine the effort, the risk, and the sheer hard labour that it must have taken.

One of Ken Murdoch's main themes is cocking a snook at authority, and another is the fun and adventure that he and his family had during the restoration, both of which are evident in this quote:

> The bank manager asked if the building was insured – we had not. He asked how much the restoration was to cost – we had no idea ... My accountant asked if a cost

plan was available – we did not have a plan nor did we want one. My solicitor advised me to have a feasibility study prepared to show a time scale and cash flow. We did not see the need for such a document. Historic Scotland did not like DIY restoration projects. Without this approach the cost could not be met. My family saw the project as good fun – and it was.[75]

However, Ken Murdoch's book was written twenty-five years after the event. Temporal distance from difficult events is a well-established factor in providing a rose-tinted view. 'Looking back we do not remember having doubts about our aim to return Methven Castle to a family house. If there was apprehension, excitement was dominant!' Murdoch's very first sighting of Methven is recalled in this passage:

> On a wet September evening in 1952 I had the misfortune to part company with my motor cycle on a road bend. Now I had time to look at the castle silhouetted against a stormy sky … Pigeons flew in and out of upper windows. Their flapping wings told me I was an intruder. It was not possible to see into the dark interior, but from the outside this building was fascinating. The tree growing from the wallhead was a measure of years of neglect. How long had it stood empty? Who owned this castle? Why had the building been neglected?

Thirty-two years later, Ken and Anna Murdoch purchased Methven in order to restore it – but with some reservations: 'To be realistic, to turn around and purchase a castle in a ruinous condition was none other than a romantic notion.' They and their family started the restoration by holidaying in their 'Kamper' van, which they parked against the west wall of the castle and all worked together 'in clouds of dust and bonfire smoke' in a spirit of adventure into the unknown. 'We had no answers to questions – how long will the restoration take; how much will the work cost and where will the funds come from; how much of the work will be carried out by ourselves?' Eventually, over a period of five years, they managed to effect a transformation of the derelict building. One of Ken Murdoch's sketches shows the progress of the building work, in 1985.

As an architect, Ken Murdoch was trained to understand building design, as was his architectural student son, who helped with the demolition and rebuilding. In the introduction to his book, Murdoch speculated as to whether his restoration of Methven was in some way linked to his childhood, or his early experiences as an architect. It is never possible to pinpoint with certainty which previous experiences have influenced our current behaviour, but everything we do is consequent upon what we have done before. Who knows which particular early influences led the restorers of Scotland's castles to follow their dreams along such difficult paths?

Barns Tower (Courtesy of Richard Paxman)

Restoration Mania

Prince Charles, as we have seen, is a great champion of conservation. In 1992, he was faced with a pressing personal heritage problem within the property of the Crown; the great fire at Windsor Castle destroyed 20 per cent of the buildings. The question of what and how (and even whether) to restore was not only followed with great interest by the media, but attempts were made to influence the process through newspaper editorials, which put forward passionate arguments both for and against restoration. The language of conservation and restoration and the arguments of the 'ruinists' (leave as is), 'replicationists' (copy as was) and modernists (replace with something entirely new) thus became part of the national consciousness via the media.

The equally catastrophic fire at Uppark, a National Trust property, three years earlier in 1989, had been followed by a high-profile restoration that was visually authentic in every little detail, down to the artificial fading of new wallcoverings and fabrics to 'age' them back to pre-restoration appearances. This was hugely costly, but paid for by the insurance company; at Windsor the decision was taken on economic grounds to make all restoration 'equivalent' rather than 'authentic'. The fascinating story of the restoration of Windsor Castle, completed under budget and several months before the original target date, with a workforce of more than 4,000 people, is told in a fascinating book by Adam Nicholson, *Restoration: The Rebuilding of Windsor Castle*.

The Windsor Castle and Uppark fires highlighted a number of significant questions about restoration. How far should restorers go in respecting the integrity of original materials? Is it acceptable to use cheaper modern materials, such as brick and cement, when rebuilding ancient stone buildings? How far into the past should restorers delve when peeling back the layers of a building's history? Is a Victorian addition to a fifteenth-century castle to be treated as part of the historical integrity of the whole building, or as a currently unfashionable and inconvenient add-on with no intrinsic value? In 1991, the Architectural History Society of Scotland held a conference entitled 'Restoring Scotland's Castles', from which an eponymous book was published in 2000, edited by Robert Clow. The book comprised a retrospective review of eleven Scottish castle restorations in the 1970s, '80s and '90s, with chapters by various DIY restoring owners, architects and building professionals; a number of the stories and quotes in this book were sourced from its chapters. The various contributions caused some ideological controversy:

Immediately, the difference between professional conservation philosophy and the philosophy of many restorers became evident. In the aftermath, the variety of standpoints of the critics themselves became clear ... while those influenced by SPAB dogma argued against the dishonesty of 'a built-in patina of age' in reconstructed work, others trained in the context-based ethos of modern conservation were concerned at the lack of sympathy of obvious modern interventions.[76]

In contrast to the overt support for restoration offered by the Scottish Castles Association (SCA), members of the Society for the Protection of Ancient Buildings in Scotland (SPABis) have to sign to say they agree with William Morris' anti-restoration founding manifesto, part of which reads:

It is for all these buildings, therefore, of all times and styles, that we plead, and call upon those who have to deal with them, to put Protection in the place of Restoration, to stave off decay by daily care, to prop a perilous wall or mend a leaky roof by such means as are obviously meant for support or covering, and show no pretence of other art, and otherwise to resist all tampering with either the fabric or ornament of the building as it stands ...

In Scotland, as elsewhere, conservation practices have changed over time, but the SPAB anti-restoration ideology has gained little ground.

In the seventies, restorers might well have been seen as one of many products of the new democratic age: romantic enthusiasts paradoxically saving and adapting against a background of large-scale town centre redevelopment and wholesale demolition of country houses. Since then, the honing of conservation theory and practice, together with privatization fears and new assumptions about the commercial value of property, has made professionals and public more wary.[77]

Michael Davis argues that architectural conservation as a movement is losing its way for a number of reasons, including a lack of understanding of what the public wants and expects, an over-reliance on blinkered professionalism and – although he does not spell this out in so many words – a lack of common sense.

The 1990s

In the 1990s, twenty-six castle restorations were started, the largest number of any decade; a kind of movement had now gained momentum. Sixteen were bought by individual restorers, most of whom must have been aware of and inspired by the restorations that had begun in previous decades. These were:

Abbot's Tower	Gilnockie
Aikwood	Kilmartin
Ballencrieff	Kinlochaline
Ballone	Kirkhope
Buittle Tower	Melgund
Carrick	Plane
Dairsie	Sundrum
Dunduff	Tilquhillie

The majority were successful restorations, in that their rebuilding provoked little controversy, although the owner of Dairsie Castle was pursued through the courts by Historic Scotland for using reconstituted stone.

The restoration of Sundrum Castle in Ayrshire, however, was very controversial. It was restored on an 'enabling development' ticket supported by the local council, and also an astonishing £500,000 grant from Historic Scotland in 1995. Objections had been made by the Scottish Wildlife Trust, the Scottish Civic Trust, and Scottish Natural Heritage.

Many ruined towers were bought from farmers, including Abbot's Tower, Ballencrieff and Buittle Tower. Barholm was also bought by the original would-be restorer from a farmer. Although it is quite common for farmers to own ruined towers on their land, few have ever gone to the expense and trouble of restoring one. As Peter Gillies, restorer of Ballencrieff, pointed out somewhat bitterly, 'They'll have one sitting in their field for years where they'll plough around it feeling it's a damn nuisance, but if you say: "I'd like to buy that ruin" they'll still charge you £100,000.' Fenton Tower

near Edinburgh, a sixteenth-century ruin, is an exception. It was beautifully restored by its owner, farmer Ian Simpson, and is available to rent as luxury catered accommodation. Formakin – Robert Lorimer's fake sixteenth-century tower, built in 1912 and never completed internally – was finally made habitable by architect and building developer, Kit Martin, in 1998 and sold. Six castles were restored in the 1990s by building trusts or local authorities: Alloa Tower, Barns Tower, Tower of Hallbar, Liberton Tower (not to be confused with Liberton House, which was also restored, but under private ownership), Newmilns and Monimail Tower.

The last, Monimail, is the small, remaining part of a grand Renaissance palace in Fife, which was originally a residence of the archbishops of St Andrews, and was restored by a community trust. The tower is now run as a charitable community whose aims are education and the provision of relief for those undergoing mental stress, with a focus on horticulture. Restoration by committee would be, you would think, less creative, more time-consuming and downright duller than the restorations carried out by individuals who have invested their own money, time and energy to bring a castle dream to life. But not so, in most cases. You can judge for yourself how successful most have been, as they are all accessible in one way or another. Alloa Tower is managed by the National Trust for Scotland and is open to visitors. Barns Tower, Tower of Hallbar and Liberton Tower are run by their restoring trusts as holiday letting properties.

Monimail runs horticultural courses open to the public and welcomes short-term volunteers to help in the garden. All are solidly good restorations and a tribute to the teams responsible for planning and executing the projects. Newmilns was also a good restoration, funded by the Strathclyde Building Preservation Trust (although it is now privately owned and not open to the public).

Ballencrieff Castle was saved in the 1990s by Peter Gillies. The story began when he had a chance encounter with author and historian, Nigel Tranter, while out walking in 1990. Peter told him he was interested in restoration and asked him to get in touch if he ever heard of a castle for sale. Nigel in turn asked if Peter had ever taken a look at the ruin at Ballencrieff in East Lothian. He had, and had dismissed it as a Georgian mansion. But Nigel told him that the mansion was built around the ruin of a castle, and that the whole site, now deemed unsafe, was due for demolition the following week. The site was listed just in time to save it from the bulldozers

Brackenhill Tower, near Gretna, before restoration

and Peter Gillies bought the place the following year.

Like the Clows at Aiket and Gerald Laing at Kinkell, Peter Gillies wanted to take the 'Georgianised' building back to its sixteenth-century roots. In 1730, the five-storey castle had been given a modern makeover with a square façade that was poorly built; it was taken away during the restoration. It took Peter and his partner, Lin, every weekend and holiday for two years to dig the site out. During this time, they found coins dating back to the 1540s, bits of pottery, the laird's pocketknife, a fine window with a sixteenth-century iron yett and bits of the original ceiling. As the work went on, the couple found more and more fragments of what appeared to be the Great Hall's original fireplace. The rebuilding began in earnest in 1994, and Peter and Lin eventually moved in for Christmas in 1996, although the work was not completed until the following year. 'We couldn't afford to finish the castle, so we moved into the top floor and worked our way down,' says Lin. This extra year's work included repair of the intricate heraldic ceiling in the Great Hall, the highlight of the restoration. An identical example was found in Kellie Castle in Fife, the moulds of which were then taken from Kellie and used in Ballencrieff's restoration by a local plasterer. The fireplace was carved by a local mason, based on fragments of stone, dating back to 1585, found among the ruins.

'If you want a way to get rid of your money you buy a ruin to restore,' Peter claims. 'It can feel like pouring money down a drain. It was exciting to source everything and piece it together, but there were lots of frightening periods as well. For example, someone would phone and say: "I've got 26,000 slates for x -amount of money" but I only needed 20,000 slates, and maybe I only had money for 8,000 at the time, but I had to buy them all otherwise the effect would have looked like patchwork.' For the first couple of years after they restored Ballencrieff, Peter and Lin rented out rooms for bed and breakfast guests and the occasional wedding. They finally sold the castle in 2006, with an asking price of almost £1 million.

Aikwood

Aikwood Tower, in the Borders, is a small sixteenth-century tower, with an eighteenth-century farmhouse adjoining at the back, which was bought by Lord and Lady Steel from the Duke of Buccleuch, in 1989. David Steel, a distinguished politician and Knight of the Thistle, was at that time an MP in the House of Commons and his wife, Judy Steel, is the author of a number of books and plays and a theatre director. The Steels lived 2 miles from the tower and knew it well. The Duke of Buccleuch wanted to see Aikwood brought back into use and knew that his neighbours had dreamed of doing so. Although the building was in a critical state of dilapidation – full of pigeons and rats, with the main chimney breast looking unstable, and the roof, top floor and windows in complete need of replacement – it had caught the Steels' imagination. They were fortunate and unusual in having a kind of aristocratic 'sponsor' in the duke, who encouraged fulfilment of their dream. They were also fortunate in having had a legal settlement that helped towards the cost of the work, along with the proceeds of David Steel's autobiography and a grant from Historic Scotland.

> For a year – and this was a remarkably short time – there was nothing but paperwork, plans and grant applications. In the course of that year, we went round looking at other people's restorations. This made us conscious of two things: one was that there is a sort of freemasonry amongst those who embark on the restoration of Scottish towers, which manifests itself in the sharing of experiences. The phrase 'don't make the mistake we did about ...' cropped up frequently.

Robert Clow also mentioned this 'freemasonry' resource: 'Various individuals wrote or phoned, offering to exchange invaluable information, sources of materials, techniques, or simply to share experiences. So it was that we met Mike Rowan of Mains Tower and Graham and Buffy Carson of Rusco.'[78] In the time before the Internet made information readily accessible, first-hand offers of practical information from other restorers must have seemed a godsend. We, too, were helped by the Carsons and Robert Clow, and by Peter Gillies of Ballencrieff and the Kormylos of Abbot's Tower, and were very grateful for their support and advice.

Unlike the owners of Aiket, Ballencrieff and Kinkell, who demolished later extensions and kept the sixteenth-century core of their towers, the Steels took a pragmatic approach and kept the eighteenth-century extension for use as office and exhibition space. At Barholm, we look enviously at towers with extra space and wish that the Victorian farm buildings that abutted the tower had not been demolished in the 1960s. But perhaps then we could not have afforded the extra building work. I remember anxiously awaiting the verdict as to whether Barholm had originally had a rare double-cap house (it did not) and thinking, 'How expensive would that be to rebuild?' rather than, 'How interesting would that be?'

The Steels and their family did some of the hands-on work: 'Our two sons, and our future daughter-in-law, also worked on the tower from the beginning, doing much of the unskilled work and also most of the interior painting.' Although the Steels had a project architect, they did not take on a contractor to manage the job, despite having planned to do so. For reasons of cost, they employed separate local craftsmen for each part as necessary:

After the plans were drawn and went out to tender, we were staggered at the difference between the estimated costs and the tenders from main contractors. At a meeting of the architects to consider them, David said, 'Why don't we contract separate trades and oversee it ourselves?' Somebody else from the practice warned that it would probably take longer but be cheaper 'and you'd probably get a better job'. Knowing that the 'we' meant me, as I am home all week and David is in London, I protested lack of time and knowledge, but eventually agreed. It was the best decision we could have made.

Judy Steel found her pessimistic expectations of the process to be confounded, 'what I expected to be a traumatic and stressful time was good-humoured, harmonious and positive'. Hers is one of the few accounts of a restoration that strongly emphasises the positive aspects and the only one to do so exclusively, without any tales of mistakes, hardships or difficulties.

The Twenty-First Century

At the start of the twenty-first century the heritage debate was harnessed by three BBC restoration programmes, broadcast in 2003, 2004 and 2006, which used a format where viewers could vote in a competition for the 'most deserving' historic building or village in need of restoration to receive the necessary finance. Each competing building was championed by a celebrity presenter. These programmes were enormously popular and resulted in spin-off books. The 'losing' buildings did not necessarily do well out of the publicity, however, despite Griff Rhys Jones' confidence that 'publicity is certainly the oxygen of restoration'. Some deteriorated further after the broadcasts, and became the subject of local wrangling and disillusionment – for example, Brackenhill Tower, near Longtown in Cumbria, which has since been bought and restored by businessman Andy Ritchie. Its proximity to Gretna Green – it is only just over the border and can justifiably be called a Scottish tower house, which happens to be in England – makes it a favourite venue for brides, and the revenue from weddings pays for the running costs.

Not all viewers were uncritical. Patrick Wright commented:

There can be no doubt that *Restoration* has been a major success. The ratings show well over three million people watching most episodes. People have been phoning in their votes by the thousand. The programme website has been filled with animated debate, and the *Restoration* fund has pulled in fortunes. Destined to be restored with money from the

BBC's hugely publicised appeal, the winning buildings can surely look forward to becoming the stars of a new kind of makeover show ... which concentrates on the historical building as a single endangered structure, and sees conservation as a wholly good cause: a secular version of church-going, which only a satanic monster would question.

Stuart McDonald, then director of the Lighthouse national centre for architecture and design, was one such 'monster': 'The way *Restoration* treats the issue of threatened historic buildings – as if they are an event, and their conservation akin to an act of religious charity – is to present the heritage industry as unquestionably a good thing. But is it?' The media certainly believed it to be so, although the anti-heritage rhetoric of the 1980s was rearing its head again. Newspapers and magazines published an increasing number of articles about castle restoration during the 1990s and beyond, which are sometimes sneeringly described as aimed at 'property pornographers' and 'would-be profiteers'. There seemed to be no limit to the interest in 'doing up' old buildings; in 2010 the BBC broadcast the series *Homes Under the Hammer* and Channel Four Television regularly broadcast *Grand Designs*, *The Restoration Man* and *Country House Rescue*, all concerned with building restoration. Almost without

Brackenhill Tower after restoration

Ecclesgreig's interior in 2007, showing clear evidence of dry rot

exception, the tone of the articles and television programmes is admiring, congratulatory and supportive of the restoring owners. The answer to the questions raised about the value of historic buildings by Patrick Wright, Stuart McDonald and others is that the media care about their conservation, and if the media represent the majority of citizens, then we also care.

2000s – Castles Restored

In spite of the positive acclaim for restorations in the media, and after a steady increase in the numbers of castles restored in each decade since 1945, after 2000 the wave seemed to be dying back. Perhaps this was due to dwindling supplies, or economic factors, or possibly because the popular movement had begun to run its course. Only a handful of castles – Barholm, Duncraig, Dunduff, Gogar, Old Sauchie, Caldwell, Portencross and Stoneypath – have so far been completely restored after 2000, although there are a number of ongoing projects that may or may not be completed in the near future.

Old Sauchie Tower, which was built in 1540 by James Erskine, third son of Lord Erskine, was inhabited until the mid-nineteenth century, after which it fell into decay. It had belonged to the Steel-Maitlands from the latter part of the nineteenth century and, at the end of the twentieth century, it was sold to a developer who bought part of the estate and restored some houses and cottages for selling on. The developer had planned to keep the tower for himself, but instead, in 2001, he sold it to Sandy Leask, an Edinburgh architect, and his wife, Moira. When the Leasks bought Old Sauchie Tower it had no roof and only one internal floor. By 2006, they had restored the tower to a fine residence with four bedrooms.

The rather unsatisfactory story of the restoration of Caldwell Tower has been told by the architect, George Clarke in series two of the Channel 4 documentary, *The Restoration Man*. Caldwell Tower was too small and difficult of access to work even as a holiday home, so permission had been sought by John Buchanan-Smith, who now owns and lives in Newmilns Tower, to build an addition. Three different sets of carefully drawn-up plans and proposals were rejected by the authorities, so he withdrew from the project and the tower was sold to another would-be restorer, who also submitted three sets of plans and proposals. Finally, the last set of plans for an extension was accepted, but the outcome led to universal outrage on the part of local residents and conservationists, and rafts of censorious comments on the Internet.

Although several castles have been quite badly restored in the past, they have never caused this amount of controversy; in this case, though, because the story was aired on prime-time television, and because the tower is in plain view of a nearby road, the restoration had a very high profile. The misguided restoration led historian Michael Davis to devote five pages of his book, *The Scottish Castle Restoration Debate 1990–2012*, to the debacle of Caldwell Tower and to describe it as 'the most disappointing Scottish castle restoration' he has seen. Hopefully, the publicity surrounding this unfortunate building will prevent other such calamities happening to Scottish castles.

Ecclesgreig Castle near Montrose is internationally famous as the inspiration for Bram Stoker's *Dracula*. The Italian balustraded gardens have been beautifully restored and maintained, and are open annually for Scotland's Gardens charity Snowdrop Festival and again in the summer. The house, however, which is Victorian Gothic with a sixteenth-century core, is still empty and derelict, and at risk of further deterioration. The witch's-hat turret has been repaired since the photograph in this book was taken, but the building is on the Buildings at Risk Register for Scotland. The photograph on page 125 shows the interior in 2007, showing clear evidence of dry rot. The condition is likely to have worsened since that date.

The magnificent ruins of Dunskey Castle are perched on a cliff-top overlooking the Irish Sea in the far south-west of Galloway. Dunskey was bought in 1998 by Dieter Stanzeleit, son of the exiled Romanian king, who stated his intention of restoring the ruin. However, it still sits ruinous and probably deteriorating, the only change having been the installation of security fencing to keep visitors out (to be fair, the site is dangerous, with sheer drops over the cliff edge). Perhaps the logistics of restoring such a remote building from overseas defeated him, or perhaps the astronomical cost of dealing with those logistics was the major factor. Whatever the case, its future seems bleak and uncertain.

Line drawing of Barholm Castle just before the restoration by local artist Andrew Briggs, 1999

Newark Castle in Fife (there are two other Newark Castles, in Port Glasgow and in Selkirkshire), also known as St Monans Castle, is another clifftop ruin that seems unlikely to be restored any time soon. It has also been bought by an owner living overseas. The Toronto lawyer who first visited Scotland in her 50s, became obsessed with saving a Scottish castle. 'The more I saw those poor castles falling down, the more I wanted to save one; they had such incredible history,' she said. In 2000, after many years of attempting to buy a tower house on Scotland's coastline, she bought Newark Castle at St Monans, but has made no progress towards rebuilding it. Newark still lies in ruins, as it has done since the nineteenth century, when it was abandoned after part of the building collapsed into the sea. In the late nineteenth century, the castle had attracted the attention of Sir William Burrell, the Glasgow shipping magnate and collector of art and antiques, and he commissioned the architect Robert Lorimer to produce a plan for its restoration. Sadly, the scheme never went ahead as the owner of the site refused to sell.

By far the grandest castle restoration project completed at the beginning of the twenty-first century was Stirling Castle, carried out by Historic Scotland. The aim of the refurbishment – as it is always referred to by Historic Scotland – was to take back the neglected and gloomy sixteenth-century royal palace apartments to the way they would have looked in the time of James V and Mary of Guise. For several years, master craftsmen and women worked on the project, painting the interiors with rich colours and complex designs, carving ceiling roundels, weaving tapestries and sewing wall and bed hangings, all based on meticulous historical research. The result, completed in 2011, is a sumptuous and stunning visual feast, which shows us how colourful and ornate the sixteenth-century interiors of wealthy owners really were.

The House of Aldie
(Courtesy of Richard Paxman)

Towie Barclay Castle,
Aberdeenshire

Cramond Castle near Edinburgh

Buittle Tower in Kirkudbrightshire,
minus its turrets

Aiket Castle in Ayrshire

Dudhope Castle in Dundee (© Oliver Bonjoch. License:
CC–BY–SA 3.0)

Muckrach Castle, Moray (Courtesy of Richard Paxman)

Rosslyn Castle, Midlothian in 1896 (artist unknown)

Gagie House, Angus

Craigcaffie Castle, Wigtownshire

Monimail Tower, Fife

Architects' drawings for the restoration of Liberton Tower
(Courtesy of Simpson & Brown)

Fenton Tower near Edinburgh (Courtesy of Fenton Tower)

Dunskey Castle in Wigtownshire

Ecclesgrieg Castle near Montrose, before the witch's-hat turret was repaired

Newark in St Monans
(© John Allan. License: CC–BY–SA 2.0)

Ian Begg, conservation architect, receiving
the Scottish Castle Association's Nigel
Tranter Memorial Award in 2013

Bedroom at Barholm Castle (Courtesy of Angus Blackburn)

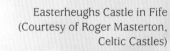

Easterheughs Castle in Fife
(Courtesy of Roger Masterton,
Celtic Castles)

Craigietocher Castle in Aberdeenshire, nearly complete in 2013 (Courtesy of Phill Plevey)

A new-build castle in Aberdeenshire

Ravenstone interior, in the throes of restoration

Lochnaw Castle
near Stanraer

Stoneypath Tower,
East Lothian (Courtesy of
Richard Paxman)

Aboyne Castle in
Aberdeenshire

Castle Wigg before the fire of 1933. It
incorporates a sixteenth-century tower

Rowallan Castle in Ayrshire

'The Highlander'
greeting visitors at
the door of a recently
restored castle

Interior, Stirling Castle

The Great Hall at
Barholm Castle
(Courtesy of
Angus Blackburn)

The author and her husband John Brennan outside Barholm Castle in 2013 (Courtesy of Angus Blackburn)

BARHOLM CASTLE RESTORED – THE INSIDE STORY

Unlike many of those who purchase a castle, we did not trawl Scotland's ruined castles looking for one to restore. We simply fell in love with Barholm Castle the moment we saw it. In July 1997, we had been holidaying at Portpatrick and were on our way to stay with family in Dumfries. We had started out the drive with no thought of buying anything more than a lunchtime sandwich, when we saw the 'Castle for Sale' sign on the A75. Taking out the Ordnance Survey map, we saw that Barholm Castle (ruin) was marked, about 1 mile up a minor road off the A75, towards the 6,000-year-old megalithic burial stones of Cairn Holy. 'If we don't go back and look now, we never will,' I said. We turned the car round and went to search for the castle. At the end of a very steep, winding and narrow road, we turned into a farmyard and there, right in front of us, was the stunning ruin of a 400-year-old tower, high above the Solway Firth, with fantastic views across Wigtown Bay and as far as the Isle of Man. We fell in love with it instantly. The walls were still standing, but there was no roof, and trees were growing out of huge cracks in the walls and on the parapet. To our besotted eyes, this only added to its charm.

During the previous twenty-five years, we had visited almost every ruined castle in the south of Scotland, where we were both brought up, and many across Europe. We had also enviously eyed up a number of restored properties and fantasised – as one does – about living in one ourselves. To fuel this particular fantasy,

Barholm Castle's west wall

we decided to look in at the estate agents handling the sale in Dumfries, just to find out the price. Barholm Castle was priced at a bargain £65,000. How could we turn it down when it seemed to be meant for us to restore? We didn't. Although had we known that costs would escalate to more than twelve times the purchase price, that it would be two years before the sale was complete, five years before it would even *look* like any restoration work might begin, six years before work would *actually* begin, and nine years before it was finished, we certainly would have baulked.

The first thing we needed to do with some urgency was to make a viewing appointment with the owner. This was before the days of mobile telephones; whenever we phoned his house there was no reply and nor was there an answering machine. At the last moment before we were due to return to our home in Holland, we managed to get hold of him and arrange an appointment to look around inside. We picked up the key from his house close to the castle, and with that visit, our decision was sealed. Chilly and dark, even in the August sunshine, the castle interior had a gloomy, romantic attraction and we could see the scope for a fantastic adventure in restoring it. Grass grew on the Great Hall floor and ivy with stems the thickness of tree trunks covered the walls. A huge crack scarred the west wall. There were owl pellets scattered around, which we later discovered came from a resident barn owl, who frightened us once or twice by swooping silently down from the parapet. Through the empty windows, we could see the sea a long way below, across the fields. Up above, fireplaces hung on the walls with no hearths and no floors to reach them.

We could see the entrances to what must be garderobe toilets in the corners, but there was no way of reaching them or seeing inside. The spiral staircase was complete to the top, although dodgy in places, and we were able to climb up to the first-floor corridor and look out across what would be the master bedroom and down the void to the Great Hall floor, which was the vaulted storeroom ceiling. We could look up to the sky and see the wall walks and the garret rooms, and had we been brave enough, we could have climbed right up the tiny turret staircase

How Barholm might have looked if Ian Lindsay's 1954 plans had been adopted

and clambered onto the cap-house roof (minus its walls at that time) to look at the fantastic views.

As soon as we put in an offer for the castle, which we did almost immediately, we started looking for knowledgeable people to talk to about restoration. We commissioned the conservation architect, Ian Begg, to make a visit and write an informal feasibility study for us.

He was enthusiastic about Barholm and upbeat about the possibility of restoring it, which gave us great hope. However, he warned that we would need 'plenty of money' and to spend at least £250,000 on building costs. In 1997, this was a fortune! Could we manage it? We were awed by the thought of finding and spending so much money. During the course of the restoration, of course, costs more than trebled. Two things saved us – one is that the value of our house in Holland also rose fast, so we could re-mortgage it to pay for the work, and the other was the generous grant aid that we received from Historic Scotland. Without it, the restoration of Barholm would not have been feasible.

Ian Begg was not the first architect to look at Barholm, and indeed the bulk of the architectural contract was carried out by ARPL Architects in Ayr, since Ian Begg retired to Plockton before we finally bought Barholm. In 1829, Walter Newall from Dumfries made a little sketch of the building and, in 1953, Ian Lindsay, Scotland's foremost conservation architect at the time, drew plans of Barholm as it was and ambitious plans for a restoration that was never carried out, using the abutting agricultural buildings as additional rooms for the castle. His drawing included two large windows in the west wall, which were never there originally, but would have been wonderful sources of light and sea views had they ever been installed.

Although we are both from the south-west of Scotland, we lived overseas for many years, so we had to deal with a battery of solicitors, archaeologists, architects, engineers, surveyors and civil servants from a base in the Netherlands, rather than face to face. Emails and competitive telephone rates made communication bearable, although for the first few years not every firm seemed able to cope with the apparently high-tech demands of emailing. As we entered the twenty-first century, more small Scottish firms began to accept the use of technology in communications, thankfully.

John Knox, said to have stayed at Barholm Castle

Throughout the restoration, I steadfastly denied that we were at any disadvantage being overseas, although with honest hindsight I have to admit that life would have been so much easier if we had been on hand. But the only way we could finance such a project on public-service salaries was because we lived and worked overseas. I had email and telephone communication with the architect and others on an almost daily basis, and we went across to Scotland every eight weeks or so once work had started. I suppose that we were no different from those brave people in Britain who decide to renovate a dilapidated hill farm in Tuscany or a chateau in Burgundy at a distance. Indeed, we were at the advantage of working within a familiar system, in our own language and within our own culture, although there was much we did not know about building contracts. Everything we did was a leap of faith and we were on a steep learning curve the whole time.

Often, on our visits, there was disappointingly little progress to be seen. If we had been there on a weekly, or even daily, basis, the frustration of seeing little day-to-day movement might have been unbearable, although I guess we would have been able to push things along by our presence – it is the squeaky wheel that gets the oil and we were simply not there to squeak much. The architects who acted as project managers, Peter Drummond and Patrick Lorimer, were on the case, chasing things up at every opportunity and visiting site on a formal basis every two weeks, however. As our bimonthly visits approached, the anticipation would build up and become overwhelming. We led very busy lives in Holland, with lots of responsibilities and activities to talk about, but when a visit to Scotland approached, all of our conversational openers were uniform: 'When we get to Barholm ...'

The nine years from our first love-struck sight of Barholm and finally getting rid of the last of the workmen, did not go smoothly. The two greatest virtues for anyone restoring a ruinous building are patience and tenacity, and I suppose we have at least demonstrated the latter. A bottomless purse would be a major asset, too. We did not have one of those, and the main leitmotiv of our troubles for the first few years was financial. Unexpected expenses would pop up like bad pennies, throwing us into a state of panic. The exchange rate of the pound and the euro (the Dutch guilder when we started) became of obsessive interest to us. Its peaks and troughs could plunge us into the depths of despair or up into a cautious degree of optimism. Our house in Holland had to be mortgaged to a frightening degree. Thanks to prudent housekeeping on the part of the quantity surveyor, the basic costs of the project were kept more or less within budget, although at an eye-wateringly high figure.

The other theme that dogged us was time. The project overran by nearly a year and a half, almost doubling the eighteen months it was supposed to take. It may not seem like much now in the grand scheme of things, but at the time it caused us not only impatience, but financial worries, as professional fees mounted well beyond the projected amount and our expected letting income failed to materialise. Eighteen months was perhaps optimistic, although not unreasonably so, as we were assured by the builders after every site meeting that things were running to a carefully planned and detailed time schedule. Towards the end of the project, when we had already struggled with a year's overrun, we found the many things that still did not go to plan extremely tiresome. I began to run out of steam. Earlier in the project, I would frequently fire off lengthy letters with umpteen points, laying out exactly what we wanted and precisely how things were to be done. I was fuelled by righteous indignation when things went astray, which gave me the energy to keep making sure things were right. By the end, however, some days I barely had the energy to make a brief phone call to rearrange delivery times because someone had mucked up when and where something would arrive, which seemed to happen on a weekly basis. I did summon up the demons of angry energy every so often to keep the letters churning out, but each one took an increasing amount of effort.

Would we do it again? Almost certainly not, had we known in advance just how long and hard the path would be. When we finished I liked to joke that now that the castle was no longer ruined, we were ruined instead – both financially and emotionally. For a long time I found it difficult to recapture that sense of adventure and fun that we felt in 1997; the years that followed were filled with so many disappointments, difficulties and anxieties. We are both experienced in managing difficult projects and juggling many complex activities, but the difficulties of restoring Barholm Castle almost defeated us at times, and we came out of the project feeling bruised and battered. Now that several years have passed and we are settled in our home, the bitterness has subsided and we can appreciate the great privilege of living where we do.

Regrets are always foolish and we now have a beautiful home, which has exceeded our expectations. Looking at the photographs of the grey ruins it is very hard to imagine how we thought it would look when finished. I do not think we ever had a clear vision of the finished product, just an idea that an amazing transformation could be made and inspiration from the restored castles we had visited. When we had a small New Year party after the restoration was nearly finished in early 2006, my uncle looked at the photographs of the original state of the building and asked, 'How did you know it would look like this when it was finished?' 'This' was the Great Hall with rugs on the slate floor, a painted ceiling, comfortable seating, embroidered curtains and a bookcase full of local books. 'We didn't,' I said. 'It just evolved.' The furnishings make the castle look like a home, but they were the icing on the cake, the much anticipated, pleasurable part of the restoration. Compared to the years of hard work organising and administering the project, the craftsmanship involved in rebuilding the south wall, the restoration of the fireplace, making of sixteenth-century-style windows, stabilising the floor, the placement and painting of the ceiling beams and the installation of heating and lighting systems, the contribution of carpets, cushions and curtains was quite minor in the grand scheme of things.

Letting out Barholm

With our financial worries mounting, we were desperate to get some income from Barholm as soon as possible. Although everything looked good superficially when we had our party, there was still a ridiculous amount of snagging to be completed by the builders and much for us to do before it could be open for visitors to stay. Every time we visited through the spring and summer of 2006, we fitted out the castle for letting. The architect advised us that we should fit a cheap 'sacrificial kitchen' because of the likelihood of damp quite quickly warping the units. Cheapness was an attractive concept to us in our financial straits, but we did want the kitchen to look substantial and well equipped – for the lowest possible cost. Most of the castle kitchens that we have visited are furnished with standalone dressers and appropriate antique pieces of furniture, and they look very well on it.

However, our low barrel-vaulted ceiling meant that we could not use any piece of furniture higher than waist height and space for storage and dining was limited. We had to have a fitted kitchen to maximise efficient use of space, and for cleanliness and hygiene for paying guests. Fortunately, a kitchen

chain store was heaving with promotional offers and provided us with a very nice, solid-oak kitchen with granite worktops, a range cooker and all the appliances we needed for an extraordinarily low price. A few weeks later, they went into receivership and I sometimes still feel mildly guilty at taking from them goods that they must have been selling at well below cost price. As an additional bonus, the kitchen units are still un-warped and in great condition many years later.

There was a lot to organise, as with any letting property. We had to furnish and equip every room. Every time that we visited from overseas, we hung coat hooks and pictures, put up shelves, laid down rugs and lined drawers to give the house a lived-in look. Beds were the most important items. Two substantial four-poster beds were ordered, one from eBay and one from the Woodcarvers Guild, along with a heavily carved wardrobe, plus a couple of nicely carved pine, single beds for the twin room. We commissioned from the blacksmith at Drumlanrig Castle, Ross Berry, a wonderfully quirky iron bed for John Knox's room, which had to be dismantled into the smallest possible pieces to get it up the final tiny turret staircase.

In the Great Hall the giant bellows table took centre stage, along with a large, dark-oak sideboard with barley twist ornamentation. It looks very much at home in a sixteenth-century room, but the interior houses a revolving cocktail cabinet, revealing its origins in the 1950s. I 'won' two huge Middle Eastern rugs on eBay and they softened the dark grey of the slate tiles on the floor. We had to buy a couple of televisions, a washing machine, a radio and several hairdryers for our guests. From 2003 on, we bought crockery, cutlery, glasses, pans, kitchenware, towels and bed linen. Apart from the antique and reproduction furniture, I wanted everything that was to be utilised by guests to be new and of good quality. Pictures and ornaments could be vintage, of course, but I also wanted nothing of sentimental value to be used.

For five years, Barholm Castle was available for holidaymakers to rent out on a self-catering basis for week-long visits and short-stay breaks. We registered with two castles agencies – Celtic Castles and Scott's Castle Holidays – and between them, they supplied us with a constant stream of visitors. We kept our prices low in order to attract clients, so Barholm was seldom without occupants. For ourselves, we had to book well in advance for the times that we wanted to stay at Barholm, otherwise holidaymakers would snap up the school holiday weeks and New Year period that we wanted. There were a lot of advantages to holiday letting. Obviously, the money was very helpful

in paying towards the upkeep of the castle. The heating was always on for our guests, and this was a great help in drying out the stones, which had been exposed to the elements and saturated for two and a half centuries. Moreover, with doors and windows being opened and closed regularly, the building was constantly ventilated, which also helped against the damp.

Despite all the help, mould was – and still is – a big problem. The leaves in our enormous charcoal drawing by Davie Burns, of local clifftop hawthorns bent double against the wind, gradually turned green, unnoticed at first. By the time it became clear that this was not what the artist intended it was almost too late. Green mould had colonised the centre of the picture and begun to eat away the paper. Fortunately, Davie came and assessed the damage, took away the picture and returned it patched and repaired so skillfully that no one would ever be able to tell that it was not the original work. We had it re-framed and the back covered in bubble wrap as a protection against the damp and it now hangs above the Great Hall fireplace looking as if it were only sketched yesterday.

Something that we had not really anticipated, and which took us aback, was the level of enthusiasm for our little castle from the visitors. Most of them wrote in the visitors' book, and all were very complimentary. Many said 'thank you for letting us stay', which felt somewhat strange when they had paid for the privilege. Some comments were genuinely touching, such as those from people who had played in the ruin as children, or a young couple who had spent their honeymoon at Barholm, or a local man who celebrated his 90th birthday party in our Great Hall. In 2009, a member of the McCallum clan was moved to write a poem in our visitors' book and from then on we regularly found verses penned by visitors, this one surely with a nod to William McGonagall:

From ancient castle in sad decay
A restored castle now stands today.
Just enter in through old oak door
To reach once dungeons on
　first floor
Once so stark and very dim
Now is a modern kitchen to cater
　for each and every whim.
Up spiral stairs we now ascend
To a lounge where large log fireplace
　and ancient rafters blend.
Up more stone steps let me be
　your guide
To a master bedroom where our
　clan chief would reside
With carved four poster bed to
　bring the eyes a treat
Complete with carpet and ensuite.
A further floor we need to go to a
　bedroom like the one below
Next a room with single iron bed
Where John Knox once laid
　his head
Up to the turrets you may go to
　view the scenery down below
This holiday must have been a
　major plan
To gather together that famed
　McCallum clan

There were a few rather alarming items in the book. Douglas, aged 6½, drew a lovely picture of the castle and then wrote, 'My little sister fell in the pond.' Another picture showed her weeping copious tears. One enthusiastic entry in the book had to be doctored with liquid paper. It was by 'The Lesbians' and the content too rude, we felt, for a book used by little children with innocent fantasies of being princes and princesses. These seven women had other fantasies altogether. We know because our housekeepers found explicit evidence of their sex games in the castle (they had booked in as a group of prison warders, but in hindsight I wonder whether this was just part of the fantasy). The Lesbians came in a very cold week in January, got completely snowed in and had to be rescued and their cars towed out by local farmers, who dined out on the story for months.

An Australian IT lecturer who stayed as a guest made a virtual tour of the castle and kindly allowed us to use it on our website. We regularly checked the Internet for items about Barholm and sometimes found pictures that we would rather not have seen. One was of a young girl sunbathing in her bikini, lying on top of the narrow parapet wall, with a 10m drop onto stone cobbles directly below her. I could hardly bear to look at it. A YouTube video showed a rock band called the Dirty Rascals in the Great Hall, where they had pushed the furniture back, set up drums and guitars and were playing very loudly indeed. The title of the video was listed as 'A collection of great musicians … and a drummer!

Guitars, Drums and a couple of beers, not a bad way to spend a weekend'.

We never met any of our paying guests, but I corresponded with lots of them and I heard their stories via our housekeepers, neighbours and occasionally saw their holiday photographs on the Internet. Although there was wear and tear and a few minor breakages, people usually left replacements or ample money to cover the cost, and we quite often gained items left behind by guests: there was a television set, a champagne bucket, several sets of bed linen and a number of paperback books. We never experienced any major damage until almost our last guests, and that was surely unintended. A couple and their 13-year-old son were booked in for a week during the coldest winter Galloway had seen for years. The water in the two garden ponds was frozen and the temptation for the boy to poke at the ice was understandable. Unfortunately, he used a long, heavy and pointed stick, my clothes pole, to break the ice in what must have been something of a frenzy. The heavy butyl liners of both of them were pierced and ripped in several places and they were drained of water. Our gardeners, who had installed the ponds, noticed the lack of water and the pole sticking out of the ice when they went round to carry out some maintenance and took photos of the damage. It cost several thousand pounds to replace the liners and repair the ponds, and nearly two years to persuade the insurance company to pay up. The larger one has a big stone installation in it and we had to hire a digger to remove it and then replace it after the new lining had been inserted. It took four men several days, plus the digger hire and cost of the heavy-duty liner. The smaller pond was well established and many plants were lost as a result of having to replace the lining. However, growth soon came back and both ponds look splendid again.

The History of Barholm

Both during and after the restoration of Barholm we eagerly sought out any information that we could find about the tower. Its early history (before the sixteenth century) is mysterious, and its history from 1750–1950, when it was a ruin, is lacking in any kind of detail. What we do know is something of the owners of the sixteenth and seventeenth centuries, and we know a lot about the ownership changes and plans in the second half of the twentieth century.

Barholm Castle, or Tower, is mentioned in a couple of dozen local history and interest books, and books about castles. While it is clear that many authors are simply repeating what has been previously published – the same sentences crop up frequently – some accounts are contradictory. Unfortunately, although most authors write in tones of authority, few give their sources. J.E. Russell, in his decamillenial history of *Gatehouse and District*, claims that the tower had been standing since the late 1400s, but gives no details as to its early owners or builders. Certainly, the thickness of the ground-floor walls, at about 7ft, indicates that this part of the building is of at least fifteenth-century origin, and possibly earlier, although the RCAHMS Inventory of 1914 claims Barholm to date from the early years of the seventeenth century 'judging by the details'.

Barholm Castle was involved in no battles and as a small laird's tower probably served solely as a quiet domestic residence. However, a few exciting events are associated with it. In 1579, the Catholic laird of Carsluith (a tower house a couple of miles west along the coast), John Brown, was charged to appear in court for the murder of McCulloch of Barholm, a Protestant, and was fined for his non-appearance. Major John McCulloch of Barholm, a Covenanter, was executed for his part in the Pentland Rising and the Battle of Rullion Green in 1666, when government troops defeated the Covenanters who were protesting against the imposition of episcopalianism upon Scotland.

John McCulloch's son, Harry McCulloch, was not a glorious martyr for a religious cause, but rather was involved in an unsavoury series of incidents, when Sir Alexander McCulloch had designs on the nearby estate of Cardoness, then owned by the Gordons. First, he 'did buy several pleas, debts, comprisings, and factories of the estate, and used all means to get himself intruded thereinto'. Apparently, this was not enough, and on 19 August 1664, Sir Alexander, with a gang of relatives and helpers who included Harry, and an armed force:

> … came to Bussabiel, the residence of Lady Cardiness, the infirm widow of the late owner of that estate. They broke into the house, dragged Lady Cardiness out of her bed and beat her until she swooned. They also wounded her son William and wrecked the house. Next year, in October 1665, the same party attacked Bussabiel, and the widow suffered fresh ill-usage. Still she would not give up her property, which led these ruffians to commit a crowning outrage in 1666. They wrecked the house afresh, and treated Lady Cardiness in such inhuman fashion that 'she within a short time thereafter did burst forth her heart's blood and died.'[79]

In the version of the story on Historic Scotland's information boards at Cardoness Castle, she was thrown onto a dung heap and left to die there. The perpetrators were condemned to fines and imprisonment, but the judgement was reversed the next day, although it is not clear why.

Barholm Castle is said to have given shelter to the fugitive John Knox as he fled from Mary, Queen of Scots en route to the continent, travelling from Ayrshire into Galloway on his way south in the 1560s. Barholm is thus probably one of the few Scottish castles in which Mary, Queen of

Scots, Knox's arch-enemy, is not claimed to have stayed. The evidence (from the Statistical Account of 1794) seems somewhat circumstantial, but it is a good story and one that is repeated in every book that mentions Barholm Castle:

> It is a singular fact, which I state on the authority of the present Mr McCulloch of Barholm, that John Knox had his hiding-place in the old tower of Barholm for some time previous to his escape to the continent. This circumstance Mr McCulloch learned from an old man of the name of Andrew Hughan, who was running footman to Mr McCulloch's great great grandfather, and who said that he recollected John Knox's signature on the wall of the small arched apartment or bed-room at the head of the staircase.

John Knox's Room is now a cosy little bedroom in the cap house of Barholm Castle, with its vaulted ceiling supporting the floor of the parapet viewing platform.

Barholm Castle was abandoned as a residence in the second half of the eighteenth century when the McCullochs moved out of the unfashionable and inconvenient tower house to the nearby village of Creetown. In 1788, they had a fine new mansion built, in the latest Classical Revival style. According to a contemporary account, 'Barholm House, the seat of John M'Culloch, Esq. is a handsome building. The design is chaste, and the approaches are laid off with much taste.' Barholm Castle became a romantic ruin in the landscape, visible from nearby Kirkdale House and probably used as a picnic venue for Victorian parties. It has been depicted by several local artists in oils, watercolours and pencil sketches, and featured in two well-known novels: *Guy Mannering* by Walter Scott and *Five Red Herrings* by Dorothy L. Sayers. Now it is a quiet domestic residence once again and it is hoped that there will be no more murders or executions of owners, nor any need to shelter fugitives in the cap house in the future.

The final, ongoing part of restoring Barholm is creating a garden to provide a harmonious outdoor setting for the castle. The walled garden in 2000 was head high with luxuriant wild growth and the dry-stone walls were collapsing under the weight of ivy. When we first saw the walled garden in this state, two biker friends called to visit in their leathers and they pushed a path through the hogweed, thistles and nettles for us, so that we could reach the bottom. In 2001, we started digging a tiny patch in the walled garden and introduced a few little plants, most of which were immediately either eaten by rabbits or swamped by huge docks and hogweed. Stones, some the size of footballs, had to be dislodged and set aside; those that were the size of tangerines and smaller were allowed to stay. What we only found out much later was that the area where we had chosen to start digging our first garden patch was the

The garden at Barholm with views looking out over Wigtown Bay on the Solway Coast

site of an old agricultural building and the soil there was much, much stonier than it was a few feet further down the garden. However, we persevered and gradually, year by year, tackled the stony soil, planted more and began to see the garden taking shape more clearly. We could only garden in short bursts, as our visits from overseas were short and irregular. But it did mean that we concentrated fiercely on what was planned; I would dig whatever the weather, even if it meant freezing rain dripping down my neck and fingers numb with cold. I probably accomplished more under those time-limited and rather desperate conditions than I do nowadays, however, when I am rather less robust in the face of vicious weather.

From 2006–11, we made some structural alterations each summer – walls repaired, a pond dug in a boggy area, a terrace built up from the foundations of the old agricultural building in the walled garden, the ground levelled, strimmed and then mowed, paths laid, beds marked out, brambles, ivy, rotting trees and overgrown shrubs cleared, etc. In the late summer of 2011 we retired, took up residence at Barholm and began to garden in earnest. Although it was a tiresome business having to wait for six years after completion of the castle to move in – and to be irregular commuters from Holland all that time – it at least allowed us the luxury of a lengthy introduction to the gardening conditions and possibilities at Barholm. By the time we started to live in the castle, we knew the ground well and had already made many of the mistakes that are inevitable in a new garden with so many different microclimates.

The garden is in a dramatic setting 300ft above Wigtown Bay, surrounding Barholm Castle. It extends to 3 acres and has six distinct areas, four of which have been laid out from scratch by us, with most planting having been done since 2005. We opened under Scotland's Gardens charity scheme (the 'yellow book') in the summer of 2013 as a garden in development; it will probably be that for many years, but with exciting potential for the future. Views across Wigtown Bay to the Machars of Galloway and south to the Isle of Man are spectacular and constantly changing. At low tide, the extensive intertidal flats of mud and sand make shining patterns across the water with the rivers and burns flowing through them, and at sunset, as the water turns a glorious series of reds and pinks, we rush outdoors to watch the sun sink behind the hills across the bay – and feel very lucky.

CHAPTER 7

OTHER CASTLES

Castle Restorations in Other Countries

Castles are icons in many European countries – particularly France, Germany, Spain and Central Europe – just as they are in Scotland, but their treatment differs according to local cultural customs, social structures, the political environment and historical events. Just as the reasons for rebuilding and attitudes towards the built heritage changed over time in Scotland, so the treatment of castles and other significant buildings, of the kind that would be 'listed' in the UK, differs from country to country and also within countries over time. All European countries have some sort of conservation body and legislation in place to protect historic buildings, but the extent to which they have 'teeth' and are willing to use them varies between, and even within, countries. All over Europe, castles are being conserved and restored, but they are also crumbling and falling into ruin.

The European restoration projects have, without exception, been on a much grander scale than the majority of those in Scotland, even though many have been undertaken by individuals; the buildings available for restoration are usually much larger than the small Scottish towers that have been restored in the second half of the twentieth century. Lord Michael Pratt's study of the great country houses (and their owners) of Czechoslovakia, Hungary and Poland after the fall of Communism illustrates the fabulous quality of buildings and contents that still exist, despite lack of care in many cases. 'For some years now all three governments, realising the potential for tourism, have been concerned with restoring their architectural heritage after years of neglect.'[80] He went on to bring up the difficult question of governments giving houses and castles back to their original owning families:

> Without some additional assets to pay for the upkeep of a big property, many former owners understandably hesitate to take on the burden, even if their homes with their contents are offered back gratis. And certainly they cannot all be turned into hotels or conference centers, as some optimists choose to imagine.

In 1991, Ferenc Nádasdy, descendant of the historic Nádasdy family, returned to Hungary in order to spearhead the restoration of his childhood home, spurred on by a newspaper advertisement sent to him by a friend that described how the Nádasdy castle, his childhood home, was put up for sale. Upon his return to Hungary, Mr Nádasdy found a castle in ruins: a leaking roof, moss-covered walls, and a deteriorated interior, left abandoned after years of neglect under the former Communist rule. He subsequently set up The Nádasdy Foundation for the Arts and Environment and began the process of raising funds to restore his one-time home. Mr Nádasdy's endeavours succeeded in elevating the Nádasdy Castle and Arboretum into a select group of 275 buildings protected by the Hungarian State, and recognised as being a national cultural treasure.

Michel Guyot in France had childhood dreams that came true (what follows is a translation): 'As a child, I dreamed of horses, of castles, of dungeons and of towers. When I grew up, I spent sleepless nights fleshing out these dreams.' [81] Guyot works on a grand scale as a kind of castle restoration 'impresario', who has restored several enormous chateaux in France, starting with Saint-Fargeau in 1979. In 1997, he began an extraordinary castle-building project; Chateau de Guédelon is a copy of a large medieval castle that is being constructed over the course of twenty-five years using only original methods, tools and materials. Workers on the site wear period clothing and cannot wear modern items such as watches, although they can get away with spectacles if they are needed. The building site is open to tourists, hundreds of thousands of whom visit each year, along with 60,000 schoolchildren on organised trips, and fund the building work. In 2010, Guyot helped to start a project similar to Chateau de Guédelon in Arkansas, USA.

Another large project in France was the restoration of Chateau de Bagnols in Beaujolais, between 1987 and 1991, by Lady Hamlyn. When she first saw it, it was little more than a rotting shell, with cracked walls, and a leaking roof, unsafe to enter. The moat was a muddy ditch, and rooks lived in one of its derelict towers. Rainwater cascaded inside, wrecking Renaissance frescoes and rotting ornate carvings, wall paintings and historic fireplaces. The cobbled courtyard looked like a bombsite: it had been dynamited by a previous owner searching for treasure looted by the Nazis. 'I thought, "This is too much, even for me".' Yet the place continued to haunt her, and, a year later, Lady Hamlyn returned with her husband [publisher, Paul Hamlyn]. 'We could see the wonderful view, and its golden stone glowing, and I knew it deserved to be saved. In a weak moment, my husband agreed, and that's where our problems began.' The project is said to have cost more than £10m, and saw 400 specialist builders and craftsmen working day and night to return the building to its Gothic and Renaissance glory, using only historic materials. The process sparked a running battle with Monuments Historiques, the French version of Historic Scotland:

We had a ghastly time with them. They had classified it as a 19th century interior, and didn't know that all these incredible older paintings and frescoes were hidden behind the newer facades. I wanted to take the building back as far as we could, but they just didn't understand it. It was a fight, because they said 'you can't touch anything'. They were threatening to stop the works, and it turned into a bit of a battle royal.

Despite the battles with the French Government (which were probably informed by Article 11 of the Venice Charter: 'When a building includes the superimposed works of different periods, the revealing of the underlying state can only be justified in exceptional circumstances'), Lady Hamlyn was eventually appointed *Chevalier de l'Ordre des Artes et Lettres* by the French Government for the restoration of Chateau de Bagnols, which became a luxury hotel. Scottish restorers also had many difficulties with government officials, but none was ever decorated or officially recognised in any way for their restorations. Restorers received plenty of plaudits from the media, but seldom get official thanks or recognition at government level.

The stories of the English, Welsh, Irish and European castle restorers have the same qualities of romance, adventure, dream fulfilment and hardship as their Scottish counterparts. The restoration of Hellifield Peel in Yorkshire became a cult episode of the *Grand Designs* television programme. Like many of the Scottish restorers, Francis Shaw had been fascinated by ruined towers since boyhood, and had first seen Hellifield Peel nearly thirty years before he bought it:

> Secret tunnels, a previous owner executed for high treason – what more could a young boy want? The trouble is, most of us grow up – but I didn't. I still kept the castle fixation so many years later, when I learned the building was available, I came up to see it again. Although

the walls had crumbled away even more the place was still magical. Fortunately my wife, Karen, fell in love with the house too.

Built initially as a defensive tower in the fourteenth century, it was adapted in the sixteenth century, then extended in the seventeenth and eighteenth centuries. The house remained in private hands until the late 1930s when the tenant died, and it was subsequently used to house prisoners of war during the Second World War, then the homeless. Its roof was removed to avoid taxes in 1948, which contributed to its absolute dereliction by the end of the twentieth century. Francis and Karen paid £100,000 for the shell and almost bankrupted themselves carrying out the restoration, despite sourcing building materials and furniture as cheaply as possible from eBay. The interior was elegantly designed by Francis, who installed a three-storey Arts and Crafts-type oak staircase and extended the attic space. Hellifield Peel is now run as a successful bed and breakfast guest house.

In Wales, Judy Corbett and her husband, Peter Welford bought fourteenth-century Gwydir Castle in a state of terrible dereliction in 1994. With a tiny budget and a very large mortgage, the young couple spent years restoring the castle, tracking down as much of the original furniture and fittings as they could. Their most exciting find was the dining room, built in 1640. The entire interior – including door frames, wall panels, leather friezes, window shutters and carved fireplace – was bought in the

1921 sale by William Randolph Hearst for wholesale transplantation into his mock-ancient castle in California. But Hearst died before he was able to install the room and it was bequeathed to the Metropolitan Museum of Art in New York. With substantial detective work, Peter and Judy tracked it down and negotiated – aided by financial support from Cadw, the Welsh historic environment service – to buy it back. In 1998, Prince Charles officially opened the restored room. Judy's book about the restoration, *Castles in the Air*, is narrated as a romantic adventure, with numerous allusions to ghosts and supernatural happenings and a tendency to personify the building. ('I was so saddened that such a venerable old house had been brought to its knees in this way. I wanted to wrap my arms around it and comfort it as you would a small child.'[82]) She, too, suffered physical hardships during the rebuilding: 'We are living in the one wing which has some semblance of a roof, but even that is minimal. In the beginning we had no hot water, no heating and very little electricity. It felt like an endurance test.'[83]

Matthew Parris, former Tory MP and professional writer, also found difficulties dogging his project when he and his family restored l'Avenc, in Spain: 'Each of us had aged visibly in the six years since we had bought the property, and the strain of keeping the project on the road had played its part ... Costs kept mounting. Difficulties kept multiplying. Red tape grew ever more tangled. Deadlines kept being missed.'[84]

In Ireland, American historian, James Charles Roy struggled with the problems of working in an alien culture when restoring Moyode Castle:

'Familiarity breeds contempt' runs the old saw, and though my affection for most things Irish remains as strong as ever, the mundane reversals of fortune that plague any substantial building project – and especially those of a Third World nature, as County Galway revealed itself to be – can strain the credulity level of any would-be zealot. Shards of Elizabethan prejudice infected my vision: delays, procrastination, financial sleight of hand, interminable tea breaks, the gush of brave talk unbacked by resolution, all caused me to think as a 'foreigner'. Moyode became in many respects more of a burden than a respite.[85]

It appears from these narratives that the experience of restoring castles has many universal elements. All of the quotes above echo the sentiments already portrayed; there is very little throughout these European stories and reflections that would not be completely familiar to a Scottish castle restorer, although the size and scale of most of the projects is far grander than the majority of the Scottish ones. James Charles Roy found Ireland very trying, but his perspective is indeed that of a 'foreigner'; if he had restored a castle in Scotland he might just as easily have found himself frustrated by 'delays, procrastination, financial sleight of hand, interminable tea breaks and the gush of brave talk unbacked by resolution'. In Spain, Matthew Parris found that working within the country's building regulations was tedious and time-consuming, as did Lady Hamlyn in France, just as many Scottish restorers experienced. All of the six restorers quoted here had been seduced by the romantic aspect of their ruin and all had faced significant challenges – physical, financial and emotional – in bringing their projects to fruition. Matthew Parris' attention to the imagined past of his Spanish castle and its temporal situation is unusual, however; nothing similar is found in any of the Scottish accounts:

Not for the first time I pictured in my mind's eye the dead generations of Catalan masovers, generation upon generation for 800 years, men and women for whom l'Avenc had been home since the twelfth century; and the sixteenth century labourers who built the modern façade of the house, stone by stone, with only mules for transport and the arms, ropes and pulleys to lift. I pictured them as a silent army, ghostly and grey, rank upon rank from every succeeding century, massed around the house like a sea around an island.[86]

The Curious Case of Ireland

Ireland is similar to Scotland in many ways – a small, relatively sparsely populated country in the British Isles with a strong sense of Celtic/national identity, and a large number of castles, many of them small- to medium-sized towers in rural areas that have lain empty and ruinous for centuries. However, the popular literature on Irish castles is rather thin compared to that on Scottish castles, apart from a series of small but highly detailed books by Mike Salter (who also writes on Scottish castles). There is no equivalent of the Collins Castles of Scotland map, which allows castle visitors to orient themselves and plan where to go. If the number of books published is a crude measure of the interest in a subject, then Ireland's castles do not

have such a high priority for the Irish and the diaspora. There are a few Internet sites, but not nearly as many as those concerned with Scottish castles – a visitor new to Scotland wishing to tour the country's castles would be overwhelmed with information, both in printed form and via the worldwide web. But a visitor to Ireland would have more difficulty in planning a tour of the country's castles, unless he/she wanted an overnight stay in a castle hotel, of which there are around twenty, or visit the few that offer medieval banquets for tourists.

James Charles Roy, the American historian who restored ruinous Moyode Castle, a medieval tower in County Galway, has been outspoken about the neglect that most of the unoccupied

Irish castles are treated, aside from those maintained in the care of the government. He is of the opinion that 'Most others lie scattered to the winds in fields and woods, farms and villages – deserted, cracking, falling apart, home to cows, pigs, chickens, mice, bats, crows, pigeon coops, peat piles, rusted farm tools, straw, refuse and plastic feed bags. The smell of manure is their hallmark.'[87] Roy does not give numbers and it is difficult to find any figures for how many ruined castles might potentially be restorable, but the number is almost certainly higher than in Scotland, which has about sixty – some of which, it must be admitted, are in the same kind of dismal neglected rural situation that Roy describes. During the Irish Civil War, some grand houses and castles were attacked by Republicans as symbols of Protestant oppression. Leap Castle, Roxborough House and Moyode House, for example, were all burned down in 1922.

Throughout the post-Second World War period, only fifteen Irish castles were bought and restored from a ruinous condition, and only three between 1945 and 1990. Of those three, two were bought by Americans. Overall, out of the fifteen restored, at least six were bought by non-Irish outsiders. This is an enormous contrast to the situation in Scotland, where most restorers have been Scottish, or have at least lived in the country for much of their lives before purchasing a castle. During the 1980s, no restoration projects were started in Ireland. This could be attributed to the Troubles, which made the political situation unstable, at least in Northern Ireland and the border regions of the Republic, or possibly because the Irish economy was in a bad state, with high unemployment, high taxes and high emigration until around 1990, when policy changes coincided with the start of an economic upturn. Yet Scotland was also in the doldrums economically at the same time. The question one has to ask is whether the weight of Irish history, in its rejection of the mainly English, rich landowners after 1922, make it almost impossible for its people, beyond a few dedicated academic archaeologists and castellologists, to see any value in the heritage of ruined towers? This is an interesting question, in that it raises questions about the value that Scotland places on its cultural heritage.

Three restorers of Irish castles, all non-Irish men, have written about their projects. One is Jeremy Irons, the English actor who starred as Captain Ryder in the 1981 BBC television series Brideshead Revisited, who restored Kilcoe Castle in County Cork as a rescue mission.

'Kilcoe was a beautiful ruin, dangerous and romantic, part of every childhood in the surrounding townlands. I shall never forget, as a grown-up child, the first time I scaled to the very topmost rampart and, with butterflies in my stomach, looked out over the islands of Roaringwater Bay towards the flashing of the Fastnet.'[88]

Nicholas Browne, an English 'adventurer', bought an enormous nineteenth-century baronial castle with 110 rooms in County Limerick in 1996, Castle Oliver, and wrote a short book about his experiences, which emphasized both the rewards and the drawbacks of the colossal nature of his rebuilding project:

> People ask do I ever wake up in despair, or feel the task is hopeless. The answer is easy – never. I love every day here, and I love the work, even mending the potholes in the drive and cleaning windows. It's the responsibility that I find difficult. Unless you are able to afford a fulltime caretaker, one that has proven themselves trustworthy and capable – which I could not afford – the onus is on you. It means twenty-four hours a day, 365 days of the year, total financial and physical commitment …[89]

The third is the story of the restoration of Moyode Castle, told by James Charles Roy, who writes an exciting tale, beautifully written, in his book *The Fields of Athenry*. There is also an anonymous lengthy account of the restoration of Castle Hyde by Michael Flatley, the Irish dancer and impresario, on his personal website; it is written in such a glowing and adulatory tone that one suspects it may be a first-person narrative in disguise, e.g.: 'Castle Hyde's rebirth … may well be the ultimate masterpiece creation of his genius, no matter what other wonderful shows he may come up with in the future.' Castle Hyde is a large eighteenth-century mansion which had become seriously dilapidated by 1999 when Michael Flatley purchased it and spent ten years restoring it 'at lavish expense'.

In the years just before 1922, one famous Irishman did restore a tower; the poet W.B. Yeats purchased and restored a sixteenth-century tower, Thoor Ballylee, in 1916 – 1922, as a summer home, although it was never a comfortable – or dry – house. He employed the architect William A. Scott to draw up plans for the restoration and to design the furniture, which had to be carpentered in situ because of the narrow stairway. Yeats wrote a commemorative poem to the rebuilding, which is carved on the wall of Thoor Ballylee:

> I, the poet William Yeats,
> With old mill boards and
>   sea-green slates,
> And smithy work from the
>   Gort forge,
> Restored this tower for my
>   wife George;
> And may these characters remain
> When all is ruin once again.

Yeats was deeply enchanted with Thoor Ballylee, but the purchase was regarded as such a folly by his friends that the American poet Ezra Pound wickedly remarked that Yeats had undertaken his lecture tour to America in 1920 'to make enough to buy a few shingles for his phallic symbol on the Bogs. Ballyphallus or whatever he calls it with the river on the first floor.'[90]

New Castles

The ultimate means of acquiring a 'new' castle is to build one from scratch, and that is what a small but increasing number of owners and architects have done. Seventeen new, twentieth-century Scottish castles have been identified; a tiny number compared to the quantity of restorations and major repair projects. The list may not be exhaustive, however, as these buildings have often been designed for very wealthy clients in secluded places and are generally not included in the literature on castles or significant buildings. Newspaper articles emphasise the authentic 'oldness' of the buildings; their representations of the appropriate features, such as significant height, turrets and spiral staircases, and even coldness, conform to a shared understanding of what a Scottish castle should be like. There are two general types of owner: the DIY builders, often on a limited budget, who want to have fun building themselves a castle in much the same way as many of the castle restorers, and the wealthy or very wealthy who can afford to commission a very special house and indulge their fantasies. The second type of owner may be divided into two further kinds – those commissioners who want their new castle to look just like an old one, and those who use the idea of a tower or castle as a springboard for a creative approach and build a 'modern castle'.

The first new, or 'fake', Scottish tower house to be built in the twentieth century was the Miller's Tower at Formakin near Glasgow, almost completed in 1913, but never lived in until 1998. It is a sad story, but with an ultimately happy-ending. John Augustus Holms, the son of a Lanark cotton manufacturer, made his fortune on the Glasgow Stock Exchange during the city's late-Victorian golden age. By the age of 35, he was a millionaire. He showed little interest in women; 'a hot water bottle does for me – when I tire of it I can kick it out'. He cared less still for charitable works; 'God help the rich, for the poor can beg'. In 1903, Holms began buying farms to form into the estate he called Formakin. And, as though determined to establish his reputation as an ogre, he laid tripwires in the woods to snare any children who dared to pick his wild flowers. Holms chose Robert Lorimer as his architect, but it was Holms himself who drove the project forward, forever introducing fresh ideas and tinkering with details. But then, in 1912, Holms fell from his horse while hunting and emerged from his concussion even more eccentric than before. At about the same time, he lost most of his fortune through his dealings with a doubtful business partner. Overnight, he called a halt to the unfinished building work, although he still continued to live on the estate. Holms died in 1938 with huge debts.

By the 1970s, every building at Formakin was abandoned and the gardens were a wilderness. In 1978, there was a planning application to build 195 new houses on the derelict estate. Fortunately, the Secretary of State for Scotland intervened and permission was refused, but it was not until the 1980s that Formakin's future was assured when Kit Martin, one of the few developers in Britain whose efforts are applauded even by the Prince of Wales, took on the abandoned estate. Ruined, unfinished buildings were restored and converted into homes in a project phased over more than a decade. The last house to be completed was the Miller's Tower, which was then sold as a quirky tower house fitted out to a very high standard for the 1990s.

Lachlan Stewart, the architect who bought and restored Ballone Castle, also designs and builds new castles; he has already built two new castles from scratch, has another new one under construction in Speyside and a fourth, much bigger building at the design stage. 'The popularity of Scottish castles has caused their prices to rise considerably and there is now a growing belief that there still may not be enough castles to go round. Consequently a new market has arisen for brand new castles, based on traditional designs.'

The 'new market' is for wealthy clients who want an off-the-peg, comfortable house that mimics one built in the sixteenth century. Broughton Place is an early example, built in 1937. The clients, Professor and Mrs Thomas Elliot, commissioned the architect Sir Basil Spence (most famous for designing Coventry Cathedral) to build them a 'medieval keep'. He designed a huge house for them,

with two stair towers, a walnut-panelled library, generous servant accommodation and more than a dozen bedrooms (the plasterwork and wrought ironwork incorporated elaborate rose and thistle designs, and the walled garden featured a sunken tennis court and a delightful summerhouse). The house was eventually divided into flats in 1975. To the casual observer Broughton Place looks like a large sixteenth-century castle, which presumably is exactly what the Elliots had in mind.

The first mock castle built in the post-war period was a DIY project – Easterheughs in Fife, a fantasy construction of two men who wanted to build themselves a castle. Between 1946 and 1950, Bill Thomas and his friend John Rhodes, who were skilled musical instrument restorers but knew nothing about building, constructed their castle almost unaided. During the Second World War, Bill served in the Home Guard. While on fire-watch duty he first saw the outcrop of rock, overlooking the Firth of Forth and Edinburgh, on which he resolved to build a Scottish tower house at the end of the war. In 1946, Bill retained the Kirkcaldy architects, Williamson and Hubbard, to translate his ideas into plans, which would be passed by the planning authority.

William Thomas was very familiar with Rossend Castle and modelled his new castle on it. In fact, many of the materials came from Rossend Castle when it was derelict, including the spiral staircase handrail, plasterwork, pilasters and fireplaces. The story of the building of Easterheughs is reminiscent of many of the restoration narratives in its epic scale, with heroic feats of endurance on the part of the two naïve building partners. Each weekend, Rhodes would travel up from London on the sleeper for a couple of days' hard labour, while Thomas would scour Fife in search of building materials. Rather than standing on a temporary platform and building from the outside, Rhodes and Thomas built from the inside. Even the roof was constructed inside out without using any scaffolding. They lifted every stone individually in a wheelbarrow and employed pit props to support the floors under construction. Finally, they had a castle that looked completely authentic, and the classical proportions of the music room, which would become a venue for musical soirees, gave it a great feeling of space. Easterheughs was bought and lived in for a while by artist Jack Vettriano. He said that he wanted to experience a certain kind of life: 'A sort of "country laird with

'Castle Dhu' built 1998–2000

springer spaniel period". But I found out it was not my cup of tea,' he says. 'I've had enough of going for country walks in green wellies.' Easterheughs is now a holiday letting venue.

The architects' firm Michael Rasmussen built Balmuir House in Aberdeenshire:

> Having already designed and extended the client's previous house in Aboyne we received a telephone call one day from Canada, where the clients had been posted, asking us to 'build me a castle'. After extensive thought and research this former Estate Office building came up for sale which had been a former Manse and by a 'clever sleight of hand' we made the Manse look like an Edwardian extension to a 16th century Tower House.

The command 'build me a castle!' was responded to by Michael Rasmussen with a cunning plan to fabricate a sixteenth-century tower house by disguising and adding to an existing building. Other wealthy clients were even more creative in their approach – or allowed their architects to be so. Corrour Lodge, for example, is not instantly recognisable as a Scottish castle, but is described as such in its advertising copy and in newspaper articles. Its Modernist towers, great cones rising from the ground, give it the 'castle' justification and stand out against the skyline; it even has a great hall and spiral staircase. Commissioned from architect, Moshe Safdie, by one of Britain's richest women, Lisbet Koerner, the Royal Fine

Arts Commission of Scotland noted at the time of review that the Corrour Lodge is 'destined to become one of the few examples of world-class 20th-century architecture in Scotland'.

Not very far from Broughton Place is another contemporary tower house, Castle Dhu, built from 1998–2000, to the design of the architect Crichton Wood. It is described by John Dunbar in the *Buildings of Scotland* series:

> Strictly contemporary design, relying for its effect upon form and massing rather than replication of medieval detail … Rendered breeze block and brick, with gabled slate covered roofs. The stair-turret rises to a glazed caphouse, and two of the salient angles of the main tower sprout metal-framed glass turrets to capture the magnificent views to S and E.[91]

Brockloch Tower

In most of the new towers and castles there has been account taken of the local context and an attempt to blend in with the landscape, along with a quest for internal fittings, which look authentic, as in Strathieburn Castle, built by an architect as a DIY project in 1985, described here in a newspaper article:

> 'They simply can't believe it when they hear the truth,' says Guthrie, an oil executive from Aberdeen. He bought the house four years ago from an architect who had built it as his dream home before retiring abroad. 'He spent years hunting down reclaimed materials: carved stone corbels from demolished towers; flagstones from a church; a sixteenth-century fireplace; oak beams and panelling. The house may be modern, but much of the fabric is genuinely old.' It was also, when he bought it, lacking many modern comforts. 'A real castle is supposed to be cold and austere, and that's exactly how it was when we arrived,' says Guthrie. 'A major renovation was required to install central heating, double-glazing and improved facilities, along with a revamp of the decor.' Strathieburn is fun. However well it may deceive, it is not a precious relic that imposes rules and standards on anybody who dares to live there.

The last sentence takes an oblique thrust at the regulations imposed on historic buildings and provides a *raison d'être* or justification for a new building. It is akin to having one's cake and eating it. The retired architect, Ian Begg, who has been involved in more than a dozen castle restorations, including the rescue of Rossend Castle (*See* Chapter 4), was asked whether he would want to restore a castle for himself, but he responded that he would prefer to build a new castle from scratch. He began, in the early 1990s, to build himself a new tower in Plockton, called Ravenscraig:

> When it came to building a new house for myself, many people suggested I get an old tower and restore it, but there was no old tower where I wanted it. Besides, I wasn't particularly interested in restoring one for myself. The challenge of seeing whether I could build a new tower and get the feel of an old one plus built in modern conveniences had more appeal. So I did … it is probably now as finished as I will ever see it. And visitors come back again. It works.[92]

The 'oldness' that both Ian Begg and the architect of Strathieburn were striving for is reminiscent of the anti-Modernist preoccupations that Ziolkowski described in his extended essay on tower living in the early twentieth century, which he described as a response to and a bulwark against urban Modernism and cultural despair. Other castle builders had a commercial reason for their projects, such as Glenskirlie Castle in Aberdeenshire, here reported in a local newspaper:

When the Macaloney family went looking for a castle to turn into a hotel they couldn't find one that quite fitted the bill. But instead of giving up, they went one better – they built their own. Most Scottish castles boast rough stonework, banqueting halls and fireplaces you could fit an elephant into – but not many have spa baths, wifi connections and bedrooms called Sexy Rexy. Glenskirlie Castle, near Kilsyth, has turrets, a spiral staircase, thick solid oak doors and beautiful gardens. But it also has all mod cons and its own restaurant.

The salient features, 'turrets, a spiral staircase, thick solid oak doors' demonstrate an understanding of what a 'real' castle should be like. The height, harling and round turret-topped tower make it instantly recognisable as a Scottish castle, even if it does not conform to the proportions and design of any existing building.

Brockloch Tower, near Carsphairn, was built in 2003–4 by a former policeman from Manchester, Dave Donnachie. It sits in splendid isolation in the wild countryside of South Ayrshire, looking as if it has stood in the same spot for centuries. Indeed, there was originally a tower on the spot, as can be seen from Timothy Pont's map of the late sixteenth century and there were still rubble footings, 3–4ft high when Dave Donnachie started building. However, nothing is known about the original Brockloch Tower and the contemporary tower is wholly new and conjectural in its form.

The Donnachies searched for authentic looking materials and had the usual problems with the weather that are common to most castle-building projects:

> Much stone was sourced locally from farmers, and a stone yard in Dumfries. We searched for good second-hand slates and found sources in Lanark with Welsh and Caithness slate. The stonemason worked tirelessly, but then the rains came and they stayed and stayed. I could not believe it, but for months it was high winds and rain and it nearly washed away our gravel road which had just been laid. Urgent repairs had to be done to save it, but the tower kept going up and up.

Phill Plevey has also had the weather to contend with when building Craigietocher Castle in Aberdeenshire, among other difficulties. He started out trying to buy a castle to restore, but decided that the difficulties were too great. In light of this, he decided to build his own sixteenth-century tower house from scratch, believing it would be cheaper and simpler, and bought

Broughton Place near Biggar

a plot of land in 1995. Phill came up against the kind of building regulations for which we obtained 'relaxations' at Barholm on account of the house being a historic monument, e.g. the need for a second staircase to meet fire-safety regulations and window sizes being in proportion to wall areas in order to give sufficient light. However, in a new build there are no relaxations, although Phil was helped by a sympathetic planning officer. Work on the tower did not start until 2008, followed by several years of extremely wet summers and severe winters, which damaged the cast stone and held up the builders. By 2013, the tower was complete to the wall heads, with a roof and windows installed and the whole looking good and almost finished, but costs had risen inexorably from an initial estimate of £250,000. 'When I now look at how much I have spent on building Craigietocher, to-date £755,786, and look at how much I still have to spend to complete it, upwards of £120,000, I think I would have been better restoring an old Tower.' Perhaps – it is a difficult judgement to make, but at least Phill will have a home that has been built to his own needs and specifications rather than adapting a building from 400 years ago.

In 2001, Cameron Mackintosh, theatre impresario, commissioned the building of a large house with castle-like features on the shores of Loch Nevis, in a mixture of architectural styles – a pseudo-medieval round tower in the centre, surrounded by add-ons that could be imitating anything from the seventeenth to early twentieth century. The new castles represent such a variety of building styles, owner types and reasons for building that they cannot be said to consist of any kind of 'movement' or phenomenon in the world of Scottish castles; numbers remain too small for generalisations to hold water. The building of new castles and towers seems to be an expression of people's desire for the security of a refuge from the modern world, an enthusiasm for times past and/or a status symbol; for a few architects there may also be a genuinely exciting exploration of the fusion of traditional and new design and materials. Whatever style is built in, however, they can be assured that people will be fascinated and the media will treat the results kindly and report admiringly. A new Scottish castle is always good copy.

The Projects that Failed to Make it

Suppose one of you wants to build a tower. Will he not first sit down and estimate the cost to see if he has enough money to complete it?

(Luke 14:27-29)

Torwood Castle

A sad and unsatisfactory outcome is when a castle restoration is started and then stalled. Some owners managed to struggle on and work at their restoration over many years in a DIY fashion. Torwood Castle, near Falkirk, was bought in 1957 by Gordon Millar, a former Second World War pilot and chartered accountant, from the Carron Company. He is reported to have lived in the building from 1961 until his death in 1998, having built a concrete dome for shelter within the roofless tower. He lived without running water or any of the comforts of modern life, gaining a local reputation as an eccentric old man. He was a DIY 'restorer' who worked on the rebuilding alone with no expert help or advice and with apparently no regard to historical authenticity. A local amateur historian, Nigel Turnbull, wrote an account of Gordon's life:

> Gordon did an incredible amount of work on Torwood Castle … He rebuilt a large section of stonework on the north wall of the Grand Hall. He built new sections of spiral staircase (using concrete) … Somewhere along the line, he learned the art of arch building and arches started appearing in Torwood Castle where arches had never been before. A room appeared that had never been there before. This was not a renovation by the standard definition of the word – more like Gordon's creative juices flowing.[93]

Gordon Millar is an extreme example of the 'hobby restorer' who purchased a castle very cheaply in order to pursue a DIY rebuilding, which in many cases could never be fulfilled. Frank Renwick of Ravenstone Castle and Patrick Whitford of Barholm are other examples. Both had to give up their castles after spending years clearing rubble and ivy, but achieving no substantial building work – although Frank Renwick used fallen stones from Ravenstone to build his own fantasy gatehouse and homage to Princess Diana in the grounds.

The moral and ethical issues arising from such unfulfilled dreams are troubling, especially when they involve changes that damage the fabric of the building. Most – perhaps all – restoring owners could be described as 'dreamers', and many struggle financially with their projects, but the dreamers without money tend not to get very far; building work requires large sums of capital and a reasonable cash flow. Despite the eventual profits that were made by some restorers who

sold on, a number of projects did not make it to completion. The planned restorations that stalled, for whatever reason, throw into relief the particular difficulties inherent in castle rebuilding. All of these were planned as restorations by owners who were, presumably, filled with optimism and had a vision of rescuing a ruinous building and bringing it back to a habitable state, like the other 130 successful projects – except that the restoration never happened, or at least not until another would-be restoring owner came along and bought the building. Many restorers admit that they were unduly optimistic about the costs of restoring and that eventual costs were a severe strain on their budgets. Matthew Parris wrote:

> Perhaps it is lucky that neither the scale nor the expense of what we still had to do had properly dawned on us – let alone the time it would take to do it. Otherwise we might have despaired ... All I can say, though, is that in the face of the major restoration of an historic building, no high-earning job is high-earning enough.[94]

Several restorers started the building work and managed to get the castle at least partly habitable before they were forced to give up. The former owners of Fa'side, Hatton and Law castles had their almost-finished buildings repossessed by the lenders when they ran out of money and their dream castle was sold on to other restorers. Niddry, Balgonie, Duncraig, and Ravenstone

Inchdrewer Castle (© Richard Paxman)

were sold on by their first restoring owners before the work was complete, for various reasons, and the new owners are continuing with the building work. Some, like Duntarvie, were begun but not completed; others, such as Dunskey, Baltersan and Lordscairnie, never made it off the ground. Rowallan and Tioram were for many years the subjects of long-running disputes between their would-be restoring owners and Historic Scotland. The restoration of Inchdrewer Castle was started and then abandoned by owner Robin Ian Evelyn Milne Stuart le Prince de la Lanne-Mirrlees – who provided Ian Fleming with inspiration for the character and exploits of James Bond – in 1971 and was subsequently placed on the 'Buildings at Risk' inventory for Scotland in 2008 due to lack of maintenance and security. Robin de la Lanne-Mirrlees died in 2012 and Inchdrewer Castle was put on the market in 2013 for an eye-watering £400,000 (considering that it is a ruin on a small plot of land). It has now reportedly been bought by a Russian princess.

Balgonie is still inhabited by the second restorers, the Morris family, and although it is run as a business (weddings, corporate events and guided tours), it is not finished and the proceeds are used to continue to finance the ongoing restoration.

Niddry is also still inhabited by the second restorers, Richard and Malin Nairn, who are continuing to work on the rebuilding. Ravenstone was sold on, in 2001, to Steve and Sue Atterton, who are still, in 2014, working on the restoration as a DIY project. Duncraig was

Niddry Castle

bought by members of an extended family, who all eventually gave up and left, apart from the original couple, Perle and Sam Dobson, whose idea it was to buy the property; they eventually sold, before the work was finished, in 2009. Theirs was the grandest dream, of restoring an eighty-nine-room decaying Victorian mansion, from the very humblest of beginnings, with no kind of cultural connection:

> 'I'd never been to Scotland before, but when we all came up to view the house, we just fell in love with the place.' Perlin's parents came to the UK from Jamaica in the 1960s, and her father died when she was young. Raised by a single mother with four siblings, she did not have her own bedroom until she was 16. 'I dreamed of space,' she says.[95]

All of these uncompleted projects had taken years of their would-be restoring owners' lives – from seven years for the owner of Lordscairnie to sixteen for

James Brown of Baltersan. As he said, 'A dream can become a heavy burden.' The vision of finishing is what kept the owners going, but James Brown never realised his dreams, so eloquently expressed. Yet 100 other owners did reach the end of their restorations. What are the determining factors that differentiate between successful and unsuccessful projects? One could claim a number of interrelated factors, to do with personality (determination, optimism, stoicism, tenacity) and practicalities (availability of access and materials, an experienced workforce, sympathetic local planning officials) but it is clear that there are only two assets that are absolutely essential: consent from Historic Scotland (or local planners if the building is not listed) and enough funds to finance the building work. Without both of these, projects are doomed. James Brown had the former, even including the provisional offer of quite a generous grant towards the restoration of Baltersan, but he was unable to find

the necessary finance to complete the building work (always a condition of a grant). Rowallan, Duntarvie and Tioram had the latter, but not the former, although things may change in the future.

Peter Gillies managed the restoration of Ballencrieff as a DIY project in the 1990s, but in 2005, he warned future restorers: 'Castle restoration is too expensive for ordinary people these days. Unless you've got money in place, you can't do it. Thirty years ago it was possible for those of modest income.' This is partly because there has been a tightening up of regulations and a more rigorous approach taken to overseeing conservation and restoration work, but also partly because building and labour costs have risen over the past half century. Grants from Historic Scotland were given to at least a quarter of the individual restoring owners and the money was doubtless more than useful – but never sufficient, without a considerable contribution to the bulk of the costs on the part of the owner.

Lordscairnie Castle. Note the evidence of robbed stone in the bottom corners (Courtesy of Richard Paxman)

Altogether, fourteen would-be restoring owners sold on, or had the castle repossessed before they finished (or in some cases, before starting). The majority of reasons for giving up on a proposed restoration are financial. The would-be restoring owner of Lordscairnie, Robert Bourne, an American dotcom millionaire, however, claimed that distance was the problem:

> He can still remember the 'whoop' of joy he gave when he first saw the castle, near Monzie, in Fife, which was abandoned in 1644. 'I visited in the depths of winter. I drove up and the ground was lightly dusted with snow and frost. I just loved it. You don't get anything like it in America.' Full of entrepreneurial spirit, Bourne, 37, founder of the financial software company Pegasus, snapped up the castle, set in 30 acres of grassland, for £80,000, to turn it into a home. 'You can't buy a closet for that in New York,' he says. But, after seven years, without a builder in sight, and more than £30,000 of research and surveys, the uninhabitable castle is back on the market.[96]

When Bourne bought Lordscairnie in 1996 he intended to use it not only as a family home, but also as a centre of excellence for Internet-software development and a retreat for software developers. His wife, violinist Maria Bachmann, planned to use the castle's Great Hall as a venue for concerts and

recordings. These were ambitious plans, which came to nothing. They expected to take possession of the castle in late 2001, but instead he sold it in 2003, without any work having been done, after he sold his company and moved to the west coast of America, claiming that Fife was 'too far for a weekend bolthole'.

The stalling of the restoration of Duntarvie Castle in West Lothian was apparently due to disenchantment with planning objections. Duntarvie is a large, late sixteenth- to early seventeenth-century house that is a roofless ruin. In 1993, Mr Nicholsby, an Edinburgh businessman, bought Duntarvie from the Hopetoun Estate, hoping to restore it as a business headquarters. In 2004, he was given planning permission by West Lothian Council to restore the castle for use as an extension of his business, for corporate headquarters and a kilt-fitting centre. However, Historic Scotland opposed the plans. In 2008, *The Sunday Times* reported the proposed sale of the building, still scaffolded but unrestored:

> As the kilt-maker clashed heads with the bureaucrats, however, years passed. He no longer has the need – or presumably the will – to see his scheme completed. He says: 'It cost a lot of money and grief to get to this stage. Buying Duntarvie alone took five years of negotiations. All the hard work has been done in terms of bureaucracy. In relative terms, the building work could be pretty straightforward. But I am 61 now, and time moves on.'

In 2011, it was still for sale after three years on the market, for £500,000, with full planning consent for restoration into a modern office headquarters/conference facility. In 2013, Nr Nicholsby obtained planning permission to build a tank play park in the grounds of Duntarvie Castle, in the hope of using the profits to restore the castle.

Peter Miller's ten years of ownership of Stoneypath (or Stonypath) Tower came to nothing, due to lack of finance, and he sold it to Stephen Cole in 2001, who restored it between 2001–06. Miller bought Stonypath Tower in East Lothian in the mid-1980s with the firm intention of restoring the crumbling structure and taking up residence. The investment required was enormous, however. Optimistic guesses suggested that £250,000 might create a habitable home, if it were allied with the huge commitment of time and energy on the part of the Millers. Spending double and treble

Ballone before restoration carried out by the architect Lachlan Stewart (Courtesy of Richard Paxman)

that would have been easy. During his decade as Stonypath's custodian, 'Mr Miller was blessed with neither the time nor the money to undertake the work – although he did turn the adjacent cottages into a useful place to live while the work was underway. Eventually, after much heart searching, he sold his pile of rubble little changed from the day it became his.'

James Brown, owner of Baltersan, tried to raise the finance to restore it for sixteen years, but finally put the castle on the market in 2008. Its large size – and consequent high rebuilding costs – coupled with its unfortunate situation, close to a busy road, with a tiny amount of ground and no access, mean that it is very difficult to market. Sadly, it seems unlikely that it will sell and be restored.

'I'm just an ordinary man from a working-class background,' he sighs, 'but I've been gazing balefully at castles since I was five years old. After discovering MacGibbon & Ross' classic, five-volume work on Scottish castles, I began scouring Scotland for somewhere I might buy.'

In the late 1980s, James found Baltersan. After a year of negotiating with the owner, the Marchioness of Ailsa, his offer of £5,000 was gazumped by a lady who offered £36,500. She could have got it for £5,500 if she'd known. In the early 1990s, this lady went bust and James bought it from the liquidators for £26,000.

A Building Repair Grant Offer from Historic Scotland was subject to James Brown securing £2 million of investment cash, which is an enormous, almost certainly unrealistic amount of money to raise from scratch. He gave up. 'I have reached my limit. I'm 61 years old now, I've cleared 1,000 tonnes of soil and rubble, catalogued artefacts, and sorted and stored the reusable masonry. I've taken the project as far as I can, and now it's time for me to have a life before death.' Before deciding to sell, Brown had made detailed plans for the restoration, including a beautiful reconstructive drawing and idealised imagery of the completed project, with gardens and enclosures. Hopefully, someone with very deep pockets will step in to restore Baltersan before it is too late. Many ruined castles and towers are also awaiting rich rescuers. In 1965, Nigel Tranter, historical novelist and recorder of Scotland's tower houses said, 'Although there were, and are, so many of these buildings, the wastage in them today is grievous and deplorable, indeed disgraceful.' A large

Fenton Castle (© Richard Paxman)

number of towers have been rescued and restored since Tranter wrote these words, but sadly, his message is still relevant today. In an article in *Scottish Field* in 1990, Tranter identified twenty towers (and added 'I could name scores of others') that were available for restoration. Of the *Scottish Field* list, however, only two have since been restored – Fenton and Ballone.

Castle Tioram (© Dale Wilkie)

Castles Lost

Around eighty Scottish castles have been demolished or collapsed since the Second World War. We now look upon this as a tragic loss of heritage, but at the end of the war, when resources were scarce and society wanted to look forwards and embrace all that was new, old buildings were seen as irrelevant at best. Getting rid of inconvenient houses that were difficult to maintain was almost a duty for some. One firm, Charles Brand of Dundee, demolished at least fifty-six country houses in Scotland in the twenty years between 1945–65; often a demolition took the form of a public entertainment. When Major Alan Gordon gifted Threave Estate to the National Trust for Scotland in 1948, he offered to blow up Threave House, a Victorian, baronial mansion inspired by Castle Fraser. Fortunately, that offer was not accepted and Threave House is now a popular visitor attraction.

The numbers of demolitions dropped steadily after the 1960s and '70s, but a few castles were still being demolished throughout the rest of the period. Lanrick Castle in Perthshire, for example, was demolished in 2002 by its owner, Alastair Dickson, who had inherited it in 1984. He was found guilty of allowing the castle to fall into decline and ignoring the need for listed-building consent to knock it down, but was fined the paltry sum of £1,000. This was undoubtedly far less, in combination with the cost of demolition, than the cost to him of making it safe and either consolidating the ruin or restoring it.

Conservationists were alarmed by the verdict and predicted that a dangerous precedent had been set that would encourage landowners to defy the law and demolish decaying historic properties. Happily, this does not seem to have happened on any significant scale, but conservation bodies still need to be alert for properties that are purposely allowed to degenerate in order to get rid of them.

It is not only the twentieth century that saw vandalism and destruction of Scottish castles. Throughout the nineteenth century and earlier, farmers and builders casually robbed stones from old buildings to construct new ones. At Barholm, we have three 'standing stones' in our courtyard that were used to prop up the roof of a Victorian byre that abutted the tower; we guess that they were probably taken from Cairn Holy, a 6,000-year-old Neolithic burial site nearby. Historical accounts, as far back as the seventeenth century, tell of local farmers and others taking stones from the graves for building dykes.

A glance at any ruined tower house is likely to show how robbing of the dressed stones at the lower corners of the building – see, for example, Lordscairnie Castle. Dunglass Castle, in West Dunbartonshire, was originally constructed during 1400–1542, but stone from the castle and courtyard was taken in 1735 for the repair of a nearby quay following an order by the Commissioners of Supply to use it as a quarry. Now only a fragment of the original building stands.

CHAPTER 8

THE FUTURE FOR SCOTTISH CASTLES

'It only takes one generation not to do any restoration and it becomes impossible. When my parents came to live here when I was five, we had to put basins under all the leaks.' Russell applauds people who rescue castles, because the buildings are a vital part of the Scottish tourist industry and because 'they need to be lived in and loved'.

The quote is by Clare Russell Macpherson-Grant of Ballindalloch Castle, whose family has lived there since 1546. Despite the near misses and outright failures described in the previous chapter and the depressing list of castles still at risk, it is worth remembering the scale of the successes. Occupied castles and towers that were ruinous or derelict and under threat only a few years ago can be found in every county in Scotland, from the northernmost tip near John o'Groats where the Castle of Mey and Ackergill Castle stand, to Aikwood Tower in the Borders and Lochnaw Castle in the Rhins of Galloway.

Help from the Authorities?

There exists a tension between professionals and amateurs, between the scholarly account and the viewpoint of popular culture in many significant disciplines, such as medicine, art, and psychology. In the world of Scottish castles, Historic Scotland officials represent the professionals, and the restorers are mainly – apart from the architects – amateurs. Power struggles between the two were understandable during the heyday of castle purchase for restoration in the 1970s, '80s and '90s. The restorers wielded power through their very ownership of the ruinous castles they had purchased; Historic Scotland, and its predecessor the Historic Buildings Council, in turn wielded power through regulations, procedures and authority over what may and may not be done to a historic property. Money was also a factor. Historic Scotland could offer a significant grant – although usually considerably less than one quarter of the total restoration costs – to help with the rebuilding. In some cases, such as Blackhall and Levan, the work went ahead despite an unsuccessful grant application and in others, such as Borthwick, Aiket and Spedlins, the restoring owners did not even apply for a grant. At Barholm, we were grateful for the money we received, but frustrated by what seemed, at times, an inflexible approach to the rebuilding – although, on personal appeal to our inspector, we did gain concessions that helped to make living in the building easier; such as permission to chip away part of the bedrock from the ground floor, in order to gain a bit of height in what was to become our kitchen. Many restorers and would-be restorers have railed at bureaucratic intransigence and occasional obstructiveness, and to some extent the Historic Scotland has been demonised in Scotland. But between the owners of ruinous buildings and those who also see themselves as their guardians, i.e. government officials, there are no clear-cut rights and wrongs or moral boundaries. Historic Scotland, over the years, has suffered a series of unfortunate public-relations failures, despite its record in supporting the restoration of many towers and castles and its guardianship and consolidation of others.

It is clear from the extracts from the restoration narratives and interviews that the restorers of Scottish ruined castles are proud of their achievements and regard themselves as having done Scotland a good service by rescuing its historic buildings. It is also clear that those who have a professional interest in historic buildings, particularly those who work or have worked for Historic Scotland, feel a proprietorial duty of care towards the castles of Scotland. Both should really be singing from the same song sheet, but are often out of tune with each other, to say the least. Feelings towards restorations – or perhaps towards restorers – were at times equivocal among the professionals and they could be slow to respond for requests for help. Ken Murdoch became so frustrated by the slow response of the Historic Buildings Council to his request for planning consent for Methven Castle, which had not been answered within a year, that he wrote to Nicholas Fairbairn, MP, also a castle restorer, to complain and said, 'My purpose in writing is to suggest the Historic Buildings Council requires some restructuring to make it less bureaucratic.' Nicholas Fairbairn replied that he was 'thrilled' by the letter 'which coincides absolutely with my experience of the HBC'. He wrote to the Secretary of State on Ken Murdoch's behalf, which brought an immediate invitation to a meeting in Edinburgh.

David Walker, former HBC Chief Inspector and immensely knowledgeable about everything to do with Scottish castles, credited supportive grants with huge success: 'What can be said with certainty is that the HBC's programme of grant-aid will result in there being perhaps as much as twice as many tower houses in the year 2010 than there would otherwise have been.' [97] This claim and its long-term prediction appear to overstate the case somewhat, although the support of the HBC was invaluable in saving a number of towers that might otherwise have become more ruinous. The grants only supplied a part of the total funds needed for each project (i.e. the grant-eligible part, which did not include internal fittings or services) and were only agreed to after the owners had taken the risk of purchase. We have met several would-be purchasers of Barholm Castle when it was ruinous, who told us that they could not proceed with buying it because there were no guarantees that they would be given a grant or even be allowed to proceed with restoration. We were told the same, considered our options, and then just took a huge and risky leap of faith, which fortunately proved to be justified. I don't know what we would have done if we had failed.

The following quote from John Coyne, restorer of Tilquhillie, illustrates the dilemma that some owners faced:

> Mindful of many of the problems other restorers had encountered in meeting the conditions for grant aid, we were reluctant to apply for the relatively small amount of assistance which was available at the time. In the end we realised that the conditions that would have to be met for scheduled monument consent were much the same as for grant aid. As satisfying the conditions would entail substantial additional expense, we applied for the grant as a welcome means of helping to offset the increased cost.[98]

There is no additional dimension of freedom offered by not applying for grant aid for a restoration of a scheduled monument or Grade A listed building; the same conditions and regulations apply whether one receives money from the state or not. Those owners who did not apply on principle lost out on what might have been a welcome injection of financial support, but at least they left the coffers a little bit fuller for those who came after them.

David Walker traced the history of grant aid for castles:

> With some 60 castles already taken into care since the passing of the Ancient Monuments Act of 1900, and estates unwilling to spend large sums on structures of no beneficial use, it had become evident that wherever practicable other solutions would have to be found for most of the other major tower houses still at risk. Thus in 1969–70 the sculptor Gerald Ogilvie Laing was given grant aid to restore the 1594 tower house at Kinkell.[99]

This account, with its clear implication that a decision had been taken to reach out and help Laing with Kinkell does not quite tally with Laing's own account: 'I wrote to the Historic Buildings Council once more … I told them of my plan to restore Kinkell. They replied to the effect that they would not be willing to assist me in any way.'[100] Laing went ahead with the work on his own, not knowing the costs ahead of him and whether he would be able to afford them. Later, he tried again:

> We were now well into the process of restoration. It continued to puzzle me that our application to the Historic Buildings Council for financial help had been turned down out of hand. It seemed to me that we were exactly the sort of case which they were expected to assist – private individuals of limited means doing their best to restore a building of historical interest without any commercial gain in view. Though the Council is composed of a group of people interested in architecture it is administered on a day-to-day basis by career bureaucrats. I suspected that one of them, unaware of the

quality of Kinkell and evidently ignorant on the subject of Scottish architecture, had been instrumental in rejecting our case. [101]

Whether or not Laing was correct in his assumption he found a way around the problem by phoning his neighbour Lord Cawdor, then chairman of the HBC, and inviting him to visit Kinkell. 'Within a couple of weeks he visited the site and was impressed by the amount of work we had done in so short a time. Subsequently the Council agreed to help us to the tune of £4,000.'[102] Laing's experiences chime with ours. Persistence paid off in the end, but it was a long and frustrating struggle even to be allowed to apply for a grant, and initially we were told categorically by an inspector that we would not be successful (we were). The owners of Cramond had the same experience. Fortunately, things have changed and applicants have at least the benefit of a much more transparent system when applying for grants today.

There is one fundamental question that underpins some of the tension between owners and Historic Scotland: is restoration the right thing to do with a ruined historic building? Among architects, campaigners and would-be restorers over this issue, there is ideological disagreement, with the SPAB position still cleaving to the words of William Morris:

But those who make the changes wrought in our day under the name of Restoration, while professing to bring back a building to the best time of its history, have no guide but each his own individual whim to point out to them what is admirable and what contemptible; while the very nature of their task compels them to destroy something and to supply the gap by imagining what the earlier builders should or might have done. Moreover, in the course of this double process of destruction and addition, the whole surface of the building is necessarily tampered with; so that the appearance of antiquity is taken away from such old parts of the fabric as are left, and there is no laying to rest in the spectator the suspicion of what may have been lost; and in short, a feeble and lifeless forgery is the final result of all the wasted labour.

Some of the restorations of Scottish castles have undoubtedly been done on 'individual whim' and with little more than a nod to historical authenticity. Although most owners have claimed to be wedded to the ideal of 'authenticity' (even if their ideas of what that might constitute were completely mistaken), a few have simply done as they wished with their buildings, to make their fantasy idea of a castle a reality. Some 'restorations' seriously compromised the integrity of historic buildings, and/ or were carried out by owners who took a deliberately anti-authoritarian stance and flaunted it, so that one can understand the dismay and anger of Historic Scotland officials, who are motivated to work there, we must presume, because of an interest in caring for historic buildings. Peter Hewkin, who bought Craigrownie Castle in a derelict state in 1996, was one such owner whose project was nonetheless reported in admiring tones by the *Daily Telegraph*:

> In the opinion of Historic Scotland's experts, the castle would cost about £1.5 million to restore; a sum that far outstripped its value, even as a finished home. Mr Hewkin knew, however, that this estimate derived from the experience of conservation architects who used rare materials and original techniques for their immaculate reproductions. He also knew that it was based on using building firms that specialised in grant-aided projects which could be priced as if they were insurance jobs. But he was not part of this world and he had his own ideas. 'I'd done up every house I'd lived in,' he explains. 'Although I'd never worked on such a scale, I knew how to source materials and labour, how to find the best solutions and how to oversee a project.' He planned to treat the restoration as anything but an academic exercise. The castle, when reborn, would be structurally sound and it would look aesthetically convincing, but the materials and skills employed would not necessarily be those available a century and a half ago. So plasterboard was used in place of lathe and plaster and the convincing stonework in the hall is actually

lime render mixed with white cement and scored to resemble sandstone blocks. Fire-doors were replaced, in appropriately Gothic style, by a creative local chippie.

A number of owners carried out their restorations without an architect, or with minimal support, sometimes for reasons of cost, but sometimes because of a belief that the owners need to be in control. John Coyne, who restored Tilquhillie Castle, wrote: 'Although the advice of experts is invaluable, one should never give up direct control. The restoration of a castle is much too important to leave to the professionals, no matter how well-intentioned.'[103] (He did, however, use an experienced conservation architect, France Smoor, in his project and he did complete an extremely sensitive and careful restoration of his castle.) In the 1980s and '90s there was an entrenched 'them and us' atmosphere among some Scottish castle owners and an antagonistic stance towards owners on the part of some Historic Scotland officials, both of which were understandable, particularly in terms of the lack of information available and the poor communication in the days before the Internet enabled organisations to become more readily transparent. The encouragement of the entrenched positions taken by the newspaper media did not help. Referring to Kirkhope, Peter Clarke reflected that the restoration 'served as a cameo of what is so difficult about much of Scotland. We spent 10 years filling in forms to get the necessary permissions – doing the physical work took us only four months.'

Michael Russell, SNP Scottish Minister for Culture, External Affairs and the Constitution, attempted to introduce a new working culture into the organisation in 2009: 'Historic Scotland involves people with tremendous ability and tremendous enthusiasm. We need to make that organisation and those in it more flexible and more open; we need to make the organisation more easily accessed; and we need to make its culture more outward looking.' He went on, later: 'I am determined that, while I am responsible for my post, Historic Scotland will be much more positive and helpful. Indeed, it is already being so.' In response to the minister's encouragement, Historic Scotland launched the Scottish Castles Initiative in 2009, whereby they put on the Internet a list of potentially restorable castles and an encouraging message to potential restorers:

There is a long tradition of successful castle and tower house restoration in Scotland as seen at Duart Castle which was restored in the early 20th century and Fenton Tower in the early 21st century. Restoration projects are by their nature likely to be complex and restoration will not be an appropriate course of action in every case. However Historic Scotland believes that there is potential for more and this initiative is intended to make the process of taking forward restoration projects more straightforward and transparent. The Scottish Castle initiative is designed to encourage investment in this aspect of Scotland's built heritage by providing advice on processes and best practices, and by offering exemplars of successful past projects.

Despite its current overt encouragement of new restoration projects, Historic Scotland is obliged to work within the

Abbot's Tower after restoration

framework of the Venice Charter and all of the subsequent European conservation agreements; it used these as justification for refusing permission for the de-scheduling and rebuilding of Castle Tioram. The very public clashes between Historic Scotland and the owner of Castle Tioram, Lex Brown, divided communities between those who support his plans for a rebuilding of the castle to provide living accommodation and those who believe that it should be left as a consolidated ruin; the divisions crossed party political boundaries and aroused anger among Brown's many high-profile supporters, such as Ranald McDonald, chief of Clan Macdonald of Clanranald (of which Castle Tioram is the traditional seat). The media was overwhelmingly supportive of Lex Brown; particularly *The Scotsman*, which waged a sort of campaign on his behalf. But the broadcaster and journalist, Muriel Gray, struck an unusually dissident note in the *Sunday Herald*, in which she argued that Castle Tioram should not be restored: '... reconstructions are very nearly always utter crap in comparison to the very personal experience an engaged viewer can enjoy when given information, the object, and the space to contemplate both. One can't help thinking this truth also applies to Castle Tioram.'

The Tioram controversy has shone a spotlight on the ideological differences in the heritage debate and also on the uneasy relationship between Historic Scotland and the citizens of Scotland; the former may have won the battle over Tioram, at least initially, but in the war with the media, unfortunately, they are often the losers. In reply to a question about Castle Tioram in the Scottish parliament in November 2009, the Minister for Culture, Mike Russell, gave the following conciliatory answer:

> It is important to recognise that when decisions are made, they are decisions for that time and within the policy. The opportunity to make new applications always exists. I am certainly happy to say that if Castle Tioram's owner wishes to make a new application, Historic Scotland will work with that owner to consider what is possible. Not everything is possible and not every individual owner's requirements can be met, but the challenge that Historic Scotland and we as a nation face is a large one.

Some owners appeared to have both the funds and the backing of Historic Scotland, but still did not proceed; they just ran out of steam, especially those living overseas. Lordscairnie, Newark and Dunskey are three castles that were bought for restoration but which were never even started. None of these three would-be restorers lived in Scotland, or the UK, and none is British; probably a combination of distance, plus a lack of knowledge and experience of the local culture, simply overwhelmed and defeated them, although Newark and Dunskey are still owned by their would-be restorers. As we know from personal experience with Barholm, the difficulties of running a large building project are amplified if one is not even available in the country to visit the site and talk face-to-face with the design and construction team. The narratives of British restorers who have taken on castles overseas are full of anguish at the difficulties of dealing with 'foreign' builders, officials and regulations. James Charles Roy's account of managing the restoration of Moyode, as an American who visited Ireland irregularly, showed candid exasperation:

'In Ireland, if you don't watch it, you can be skinned alive. One of my biyearly trials was to have people come over to Moyode to discuss the job. The hurricanes of talk I endured! The mountains of pledges, promissory notes, drawings, and quotations that never materialised! The baits and traps strewn in conversation! In over twenty years, I never met a builder I thought I could trust.'[104]

Roy sold Moyode in 2008, before the restoration was fully finished.

Is it Worth it?

One question that may be dodged by passionate restoring owners is 'was it worth it?' In our case, which was not at all unusual, we were very quickly in too deep to extricate ourselves easily. As the value of the Dutch guilder fell against the pound (our salaries were paid in guilders, but we paid the builders in pounds sterling, of course) we often discussed anxiously whether or not we could afford to carry on. The reply we came up with was that we could not afford not to. Too much had been committed, both financially and emotionally, to let us back gracefully out. Dean and Miers claimed that the sellers made a profit when they sold on:

Often these restorations began as labours-of-love rather than commercial investments but the sheer romance of living in a Scottish tower house has ensured that most of the pioneers have seen a healthy increase in the

value of their tower houses and enabled them to more than cover their costs when they have sold.[105]

However, David Walker claimed that 'Experience has shown time after time that the cost of restoring a roofless or badly decayed tower house is likely to be far in excess of the market value of the end result.'[106] Who is correct? Well, Walker is almost certainly correct if one looks at the costs compared to the resale value at the time of the restoration, but with property prices having risen almost inexorably in the post-war years, it is sometimes only a matter of a few years before the market value exceeds the investment, particularly if the rebuilding has involved cost-saving DIY. Both Abbot's Tower and Ballencrieff were bought as dilapidated ruins with small amounts of land from farmers in 1989. Both restorations were DIY projects, with the owners and their families carrying out much of the work themselves. When the restoring owners sold, in 2004 and 2006 respectively, they doubtless made some financial profit – although it was certainly not 'easy money', but rather at the cost of several years of exhausting hard labour and privation, and initial high-risk investment.

Worth is not only financial, however. Abbot's Tower and Ballencrieff are among the many Scottish castles that might otherwise have continued to deteriorate, some even beyond the point of no return, that are now lived in or regularly used. Inevitably, some restorations, especially the early ones, are far from perfect and several have involved the destruction of parts of the buildings that seemed at the time unfashionable or simply inconvenient, although some additions had deteriorated past the point of saving.

Lochnaw Castle near Stranraer, ancestral home of the Agnew family, is situated in a glorious position overlooking the 47-acre loch after which it is named, in a 300-acre wooded estate near to the sea. Both Queen Victoria and Winston Churchill visited Lochnaw. The climate in the far south-west of Scotland is mild and the scenery in the Rhins of Galloway spectacular. But it is isolated and in a sparsely populated region – the easiest way to get to London is to take a ferry to Belfast in Ireland and fly from there. Lochnaw was built as a simple square tower in the fifteenth century, then large extensions were added in 1663, 1704, 1820 and 1882. By the twentieth century, its size was impossibly huge and some of the additions were demolished in the 1950s. It subsequently changed hands several times, becoming a guest

Enormous Aboyne Castle, probably at the end of the nineteenth century

house and home to an Australian cult. One prospective restorer bought it in the 1990s, but put it back on the market soon afterwards. The current owners have spent a great deal of time and money carefully and respectfully restoring the castle since 2000, and it is now a manageable home with many original features. They have ingeniously used the remains of a completely derelict Victorian wing as a walled garden, with windows and a viewing platform, adjoining the house.

Aboyne Castle in Aberdeenshire, home of the Earls of Huntly, had also become unmanageably huge by the 1950s. The footprint of the house, with all of its many additions, was well over an acre, and it was considerably reduced in size by the current Marquess of Huntly when he restored the derelict building to a habitable state in the 1980s, using Ian Begg as his architect.

Has the end justified the means in every case? The moral question of whether to change a ruin through restoration was worried at by Matthew

Gelston Castle, a consolidated ruin

Parris, who bought a large ruinous Renaissance castle in Spain, l'Avenc, with his family in 1998:

> When you restore a ruin you kill something fragile: a soul breaks free and flies away. All these years l'Avenc had had itself to itself, and now we were barging in with Caterpillar tractors. We thought to come as rescuers, and so we did; but we were also interlopers. We had come to interrupt a building's unhurried and passionate embrace with death; to break its solitude, to spoil its abandon. We had come to wreck the wreck.[107]

These words, which seem at face value entirely reasonable and uncontroversial, were almost certainly politically motivated in the context of the 'battle' against the restoration of Castle Tioram. The decision to restore a ruin raises complex questions involving motivation, representation, wherewithal, historicity, authenticity, integrity and continuity. These are rarely explicitly raised by the owner when a ruined building is restored (apart from authenticity, as was seen in Chapter 2), although when Historic Scotland is involved in granting permissions and guiding the restoration there is a greater chance that the process is examined with an eye at least on the last four. But then there is also a greater chance that entrenched ideological stances will be taken, leading to the combative obstructiveness that has not served well in the past.

Politics and Castles at Risk

There has been something of a turnaround in Historic Scotland's attitude towards restorers in recent years, from apparent lack of support to welcoming encouragement, which means that castle restoration may become more accessible to potential restorers, bureaucratically at least. As the guardian of the historic built environment, Historic Scotland must hold restorers to account, and stick to the spirit, at least, of the various European conservation conventions; but judging when to offer helpful advice and when to use authority flexibly is tricky for a large organisation bound by rules and procedures and prone to ideological partisanship.

However, the next decades may not see such a positive future for ruined and derelict Scottish castles, particularly if recent economic changes mean a slow down in financial markets and an ensuing atmosphere of austerity leads to changed priorities that negatively affect the care of historic buildings. The castles and towers currently at risk will not survive much longer without restoration or consolidation. But at least the 'SPABite' doctrine, which was embraced by some Historic Scotland inspectors up until the 1990s, seems to have become discredited. Here it is spelled out in this quote of 1900 by Ruskin:

Do not let us talk then of restoration. The thing is a Lie from beginning to end. You may make a model of a building as you may

of a corpse, and your model may have the shell of the old walls within it as your cast might have the skeleton, with what advantage I neither see nor care: but the old building is destroyed, and that more totally and mercilessly than if it had sunk into a heap of dust, or melted into a mass of clay.[109]

This is Victorian rhetoric, adducing moral arguments to forward the conservationist cause. Calling the debate a moral one may invest it with more gravitas than it deserves, however – these are buildings after all, and not people, no matter how often they are personified in literature. But the question of whether ruinous historic buildings should be rebuilt and reoccupied is still a vexed one, with the controversial cases of Castle Tioram and Rowallan Castle exemplifying the continuing debate. Historic Scotland's recent Scottish Castle Initiative and its new publications may signal a politically driven change in the organisation's philosophy, but the real test will be its behaviour and practice in the future.

During the early part of the post-Second World War period, more than seventy castles were demolished, the majority quite needlessly, but from 1975 on, castles benefited from the increasing appreciation and protection of historic buildings in Scotland and the UK and Europe. Predicting the future is a very dangerous sport, as the past is a poor predictor, but, unless some major nationwide catastrophe occurs, it is difficult to imagine the castles of Scotland that have already been restored and repaired returning to their vulnerable state. There may be less money and even less will to restore historic buildings in the future, but the work that has already been done to restore and substantially repair over 200 buildings since the Second World War seems likely to endure, if for no other reason than that they have become valuable commodities in the housing market.

Castles as Commodities

In the past, castles changed hands relatively rarely and then usually within a rarefied circle of wealthy landed gentry and aristocracy, with the occasional incursion by the nouveau riche. But among the castles bought as restoration projects by individuals, it is a surprising fact that over 50 per cent were subsequently sold by their restorers. Indeed, in the 1980s, seventeen out of the eighteen castles restored were either later sold or at least put on the market.

It seems that the dream of restoring a ruin and living in a castle does not necessarily extend for a lifetime; ownership is transient in a way that it rarely was before the 1950s. Perhaps this is because a castle restoration is a project from which many owners want to move on after a few years. The new owners do not have generations of family history to tether them to their castles and their children do not always want to live their lives in what might never have been their childhood home. I cannot imagine our student daughter, who is based in London, ever wanting to move into our rather remote tower house – but perhaps in twenty years' time she will view it differently. Whatever she chooses, it is not a matter of great emotional concern to us to have Barholm in the family for succeeding generations. If it is eventually sold on to new owners, so be it.

Only half a dozen restored castles have so far been passed on to the next generation: Balbithan, Castle Stalker, Barscobe, Cramond, Rusco and Aikwood, although more may be added to the list as time goes on. Of these, Castle Stalker and Rusco are 'family heritage' castles, where the owner was buying back a building that had once belonged to the family. Continuity would, therefore, count much more than normally. Barscobe Castle, a small sixteenth-century tower house, is part of a large estate that has passed through the family since the death of Sir Hugh Wontner and has other houses within its boundaries. John McMurtie of Balbithan took over the castle with his wife after his mother, Mary, retired.

A tower or castle is often not a convenient place to live, with lots of stairs, small windows giving very little natural light, high maintenance costs and problems with damp, plus the weight of responsibility that goes with caring for an iconic ancient monument. It is hardly surprising if owners eventually decide that the drawbacks outweigh the benefits, especially once they grow older and less fit, and that their offspring might come to the same conclusion when offered the place. Lord and Lady Steel moved out of Aikwood Tower, which they had restored in the 1990s, when it became difficult for them to manage; their son Rory does not live in it, but now runs it as an upmarket events venue. Forter Castle remains with the Pooley family, but it was put up for sale a few years ago, then withdrawn after some time. It is now for rent as a holiday let.

Conservation and heritage protection alone, while necessary, is not always sufficient; safety comes also from the economic value placed on towers and castles. The commodification in the housing market and the realities of commercial holiday letting and events – in particular weddings – has been the saving of many a Renaissance building and we should not be sniffy about this. Pragmatism, in this uncertain economic climate, rules.

Currently, Scottish castles are increasingly part of the high-end housing stock, publicly advertised for sale by estate agents such as Savills, Strutt & Parker and Knight Frank, and bought by a mix of successful business people, rich celebrities and overseas buyers attracted by Scotland's romantic past and also its lax property laws and lucrative sporting estates. In the future, it seems likely that those castles that have been restored since the Second World War will remain in good order, provided that the top-end housing market in Scotland at least holds it value. They may be joined by others that are currently at risk, either as consolidations or rebuilt as homes – but only if they are in attractive and accessible locations, which in practice means a relatively small number. David Walker is probably correct in his prediction that '... inevitably the era of tower-house restoration is drawing towards its close for the very simple reason that the number of towers capable of restoration and available for purchase is now so limited'.[110] However, because of the position of increasing numbers of Scottish castles as commodities in the housing market, rather than as physical expressions of ancient lineage, more are likely to be exchanged between wealthy buyers rather than deteriorate from generation to generation of old families with decreasing resources. Those who want to purchase a Scottish castle to live in will always have a choice of buildings to buy, since at any time there are usually around a dozen for sale – but nearly always at a price tag of over £1 million, unless the parcel of ground is tiny and/or the situation miserable. Although such prices place most castles well beyond the reach of all but the wealthiest buyers, if owners have spent a seven-figure sum on a castle home, it is likely that they will at least make sure that the roof does not leak and the fabric of the building is well maintained. On these terms, the foreseeable future for most of Scotland's castles – the inhabited ones, at least – looks relatively rosy and secure. However, there is no room for complacency.

Castles Ongoing

Several derelict castles are ongoing projects: Johnstone Castle was started in 2004, Ravenstone, in Wigtownshire, is slowly being restored while its owners live in the habitable rooms and Balintore Castle, a derelict gothic mansion in Angus with fifty rooms, was bought in 2008 by David Johnstone, who is set to become another long-term impoverished restorer prepared to suffer privation. He spent the first summer camping out in the castle's former laundry until concerned friends persuaded him to live on the castle site in a caravan. He then had to collect rainwater to wash his dishes, and take showers at work.

David explains his motivation for embarking on this gargantuan project:

> To take on the restoration of a large Grade A building as an individual of particularly modest means is on the face of it insane. However, it is one of the most calculated things I have ever done. I could write pages on my motivations but suffice it to say that the restoration is pretty much the key to my 'lock' of what I think is important in life. You may think that once the reality of such a project hits (two years in a miniscule caravan wasn't fun)

that I would be demoralised and flee. Others have indeed flown and many have doubted and criticised. But my commitment and enthusiasm remain.

Gelston Castle in Kirkcudbrightshire is a late Georgian fantasy castle that fell into ruin just after the Second World War, when its roof was removed to avoid paying rates. It is not feasible as a restoration project, but the owner of Gelston is doing his best to consolidate the structure and keep it safe as a romantic

Ardstinchar Castle

ruin in the landscape. Without the work he has done recently, the building would almost certainly head for collapse within the next few years.

The sixty castles that are in the care of the Secretary of State for Scotland and looked after by Historic Scotland are all safe from deterioration and are mostly open to the public, with interpretation boards and guidebooks available. The Ancient Monuments Act of 1900 was significant for the subsequent security of ruined castles – the first acquisitions were made in 1906 and Thomas Ross, of MacGibbon and Ross, became one of the first inspectors.

Between 1906 and 2000, sixty castles were taken into care, the majority in the 1930s and '50s. By 1934 thirty-three were in care, listed in a specially compiled article for the readers of *SMT magazine* ('A Monthly Magazine For All Who Travel By Road Or Rail'), which stated that 'In presenting this volume to our readers we venture to express the hope that it will inspire in them a desire to visit and become intimate with the many ancient buildings in which Scotland is so rich.' The democratising of access to Scottish castles was beginning, but initially only to the ruinous properties.

Castles Still at Risk

The Buildings at Risk Register lists sixty castle and tower ruins, all in private hands, which are at serious risk of further decay and even collapse. In a country that prides itself on its cultural built heritage – and in particular, castles – this is a national scandal. Not all of the castles on that list are candidates for restoration, but approximately 25 per cent might be suitable for reoccupation and the rest need at least consolidation as ruins. The list is not necessarily comprehensive. In south-west Scotland, Ardstinchar Castle in Ayrshire, for example, has a 'keep out – danger' notice posted at the railing where people routinely climb over to trek up to this dramatic crumbling ruin with stunning views over the Ayrshire coast to the volcanic island of Ailsa Craig.

Trees growing through the walls block access to the interior and threaten to pull apart the remaining stonework, just as is the case with its near neighbour at Lendalfoot, Carleton Castle. Neither of these castles is on the At Risk Register.

In Dumfries and Galloway, two castles that stand in the grounds of holiday caravan parks are at serious risk of further decay and collapse. One is Cassencarie, near Creetown, a fine, sixteenth-century tower with Victorian additions, still occupied until the 1960s and now in a perilous state.

The other is Hoddom Castle, another sixteenth-century tower with eighteenth- and nineteenth-century additions, which was requisitioned by the military during the Second World War and never reoccupied. Within

20 miles of our home at Barholm Castle there are another five castles that are ruinous and at serious risk of further decay. Castle Wigg was burned out in a fire of 1933; before that it was a fine, Georgian mansion with a sixteenth-century tower tucked away in the rear corner. Now it continues to decay and there is little prospect of any rescue, as it has become part of a working farm.

Castle Stewart, near Newton Stewart, is in private ownership and has been propped up with scaffolding for years, but nothing has been done. It is also right beside a working farm. Garlies Castle, ancient seat of the Earls of Galloway, is an isolated ruin, with little left to show of what was once an extremely grand Renaissance dwelling house. Sanquhar Castle, once visited by Mary Queen of Scots, and almost restored by the fabulously wealthy 3rd Marquess of Bute at the end of the nineteenth century (the work stopped upon his death, in 1900) has been vandalised in recent years and is at serious risk of further collapse. Kenmure Castle in Galloway is another large ruined castle with series of additions that make it difficult to assess. It stands in a wonderful position overlooking Loch Ken, crumbling a little bit more each year and looking as if it has been a ruin for centuries.

Tragically, a bent television aerial hanging over the roof shows that it is only a few years since it was in use as a hotel. Its large size, complex architecture and isolated position make is unlikely that it will be inhabited again in the foreseeable future. Many of the fine features

Cassencarie Castle

Castle Wigg in 2013

were sold off in the 1960s when the building was stripped; a distinguished local architect, Antony Wolffe, told me that he had bought one of Kenmure's fine fireplaces when the interior fittings were sold off, and fitted it into a building he was restoring. Roofless, it will only continue to deteriorate. These are the castles in my neighbourhood, that I know well. Throughout Scotland, the same sad story is repeated in every region. Redcastle on the Black Isle, Mearns Castle in East Renfrewshire, Fairbairn Tower at Muir of Ord in Ross, Crossbasket Castle in South Lanarkshire and many others are all in desperate need of money and commitment before they crumble further.

What the future holds for the castles still at risk of collapse can only be guessed in the current uncertain economic climate. It would be comforting to think they could all at least be secured from further degeneration, but that would require a great deal of financial investment for very little economic return. The value we place upon our ancient monuments is a reflection of the values we hold as a society; anguished cries about saving our cultural heritage may signal good intentions, but the road to hell is said to be paved with them. To quote another rather hackneyed old saying, fine words butter no parsnips! What Scotland's decaying castles need is money by the bucketload, investment and security. Will the Scottish Government be able to provide that? It seems unlikely at present.

However, dedicated/determined individuals and community groups can sometimes work miracles. In the village of Portencross, in Ayrshire, residents formed the campaigning group Friends of Portencross Castle (FOPC) when the ruined Portencross Castle was put up for sale by British Nuclear Fuels Ltd (BNFL) in 1998. They fought a vigorous and finally successful campaign against the sale of the castle to an individual buyer, determined to have it in community ownership and accessible to all. I have to admit that when I heard at the time that they were holding coffee mornings to raise funds for the restoration of the castle I thought they were doomed to failure – it would take an unimaginable number of local fundraising events to cover the enormous costs involved. However, in 2005,

Kenmure Castle

Hoddom Castle

FOPC took ownership and initiated a determined search to find funding for its repair. The construction work on Portencross Castle began in earnest in 2007, when FOPC were awarded grant support from the Heritage Lottery Fund, Historic Scotland and the Architectural Heritage Fund. In 2010, the restoration of Portencross Castle was completed, a triumph for the local campaigners and fundraisers. It is now open for visitors and hosts exhibitions, art shows and public and private events, all run by volunteers.

Sorbie Tower, which was gifted to the Hannay clan in 1965, is currently facing similar challenges over its future. Clan Chief David Hannay has been spearheading plans for the eventual restoration of the ruined sixteenth-century tower house. In 2001 and 2005, grants were obtained from the Heritage Lottery Fund with partnership funding from the clan and Historic Scotland. This enabled the tower to be scaffolded, so that the wall heads could be capped with lime mortaring and steel beams inserted to prevent further internal collapse, but unfortunately, it now seems that these may be causing more problems than they have solved for Sorbie. The way ahead is not clear, but David Hannay remains determined to save Sorbie for the Hannay Clan and keep it open for the benefit of the public.

In the last quarter of the sixteenth century, Timothy Pont, the talented Scottish cartographer, surveyed all the shires and islands of Scotland. His maps were extraordinarily detailed and accurate and much of what we know about the history of Scottish castles and towers can be attributed to his skills. On one small section of his map Gallovidia Pars Media (central Galloway) three towers can be seen: Barholm ('Barhoom'), Carsluith ('Karsluyith') and Cassencarie ('Kassinkary'). The first has been restored from a ruin, the second is a consolidated ruin in the care of the state and open to the public, and the third is in terrible danger of collapse. These three buildings within a few miles of each other are representative of the state of castles right across Scotland, and it is the third category that is desperately in need of help. Will the deteriorating castles at Sanquhar, Redcastle, Fairbairn etc. also be saved by dedicated groups of individuals? Or will they go the way of Cathcart, Drumrie, Elphinstone and many others that were demolished or collapsed, and slip away forever? It is up to all of us who care about Scotland's castles to take steps to save those still at risk. In the words of Francis Bacon in 1623, 'it is a reverend thing, to see an ancient castle or building, not in decay.'[III]

Sorbie Tower

NOTES

Chapter 1

1   Bevan, pp.11–2
2   France Smoor, 'Tilquhillie Castle' in Clow, p.58
3   Charles McKean, *The Scottish Chateau* (2004), preface to 2nd edition
4   *Scotland's Ancient Heritage* (1934), Foreword
5   Laing, *Kinkell*, p.150
6   Macneil, p.170
7   Laing, p.169
8   Corbett, p.59
9   Parris, p.103
10 Browne, pp.46–7

Chapter 2

11 Davis, *Scots Baronial: Mansions and Castle Restorations in the West of Scotland* (1996), Frontispiece
12 *Ibid.*, p.168
13 Rosenberg, p.7
14 MacGibbon and Ross, Vol. 1, Preface, p.7
15 Walker, p.431
16 www.scottisharchitects.org.uk
17 McKean, *Scottish Chateau*, p. 260
18 MacGibbon and Ross, Vol. 1, Preface, p.7
19 Scott-Moncrieff, p.66
20 Lindsay, *The Castles of Scotland*, p.102
21 Taylor, p.305
22 Ranald MacInnes, "Rubblemania": Ethic and Aesthetic in Scottish Architecture', *Journal of Design History* (1996), Vol. 9, No. 3, p.145
23 Queen Marie of Roumania, Chapter 15, 'Brana the Beloved'
24 Nikolaus Pevsner, *Derbyshire* (1978), Penguin Books, Harmondsworth, 2nd edition, p.221
25 Quoted in Christopher Woodward, *In Ruins*, p.13
26 The building – and subsequent collapse – of Fonthill Abbey's 300 ft tower in 1801 is described by Simon Thurley in Chapter 2 of *Lost Buildings of Britain*

Chapter 3

27 Tom Craig, 'Fawside Castle' in Clow, p.123
28 Corbett, *Castles in the Air*, p.13
29 Browne, *Castles and Crocodiles*, p.15
30 Parris, p.4
31 James Charles Roy, *The Back of Beyond* (2004), Westview Press, Oxford, p.11
32 Saddlemyer, *Becoming George: The Life of Mrs W.B. Yeats* publisher's blurb
33 Macneil, *Castle in the Sea*. P.159
34 *Ibid.*, p.171
35 Davis, *Scottish Baronial*, p.57
36 Nicholas Maclean-Bristol, *From Clan to Regiment*, p.663
37 *Ibid.*, p. 665
38 Graham Carson, *'Rusco Tower'* in Clow, p.161
39 *Ibid.*, p.165
40 James Charles Roy, *The Fields of Athenry*, pp.125–6
41 Mike Rowan, *'Mains Castle'* in Clow, p.148
42 *Ibid.*, p.152
43 *Ibid.*, p.156
44 Fairbairn, *A Life is Too Short*, pp.166–7
45 Astaire et al, *Living in Scotland*, p.110

Chapter 4

46 Astaire et al., *Living in Scotland*, p.40
47 John Harris, *No Voice from the Hall: Early Memories of a Country House Snooper*
48 Christian Miller, *A Childhood in Scotland*
49 Merlin Waterson (ed.), *The Country House Remembered* (1985), p.242
50 Marc Ellington, 'Tower House Restoration in Scotland' in J.S. Smith (ed.), *North East Castles: Castles in the Landscape of North East Scotland* (1990), Aberdeen University Press, Worcester, p.80
51 'Kinkell Castle', *Scots Magazine*, 29 July 2008 edition, www.usscots.com
52 Laing, p.94
53 *Ibid.*, p.124
54 *Ibid.*, p.149

55 *Ibid.*, pp.166–7
56 Walker in Clow, p.22
57 Cornforth, p.121
58 Strong, p.140
59 European Charter of the Architectural Heritage, adopted by the Council of Europe, October 1975, under principle 2
60 Gow, *Scotland's Lost Houses* p.13
61 Tranter, Vol. 2, Preface, p.6
62 ———, Vol. 1 (1962), p.7
63 Gifford, *Fife*, p.113
64 Kelsall and Harris, p.3
65 Tranter, Vol. 2, p.6
66 Eric Jamieson, 'The rebuilding of Cramond Tower', *SCA Journal*, Issue 11
67 *Ibid.*
68 *Ibid.*

Chapter 5

69 Patrick Cormack, pp.49–50
70 Wright, p.12
71 Robert Hewison, *The Heritage Industry: Britain in a Climate of Decline* (1987)
72 The full text of the speech is available on the Prince of Wales' website, www.princeofwales.gov.uk
73 Charles, Prince of Wales, *A Vision of Britain: A Personal View of Architecture*

74 Lorna Martin, 'Father, Daughter Hunted by Heritage Watchdog', *Glasgow Herald*, 10 August 2002 edition
75 Ken Murdoch, *Methven Castle*
76 Michael Davis, 'Castle Tioram and the Restoration Debate' in *Clow*, p.64
77 Davis in *Clow*, p.193
78 Clow in *Clow*, p.99

Chapter 6

79 Sir Herbert Maxwell, *A History of Dumfries and Galloway* (1896), pp.292–3

Chapter 7

80 Lord Michael Pratt, p.8
81 Michel Guyot, *J'ai rêvé d'un château* (2007), Éditions Jc Lattès, p.14
82 Corbett, p.24
83 *Ibid.*, p.5
84 Parris, pp.99–100
85 Roy, p.2
86 Parris, p.218
87 James Charles Roy, *The Fields Of Athenry*, p.6
88 Jeremy Irons, 'Let's Bring A Bit of Warmth To West Cork', *The Irish Times*, 30 May 2001 edition
89 Browne, p.46–7
90 Ziolkowski, *The View from the Tower*, p.49

91 Kitty Cruft, John Dunbar and Richard Fawcett, *Borders* ('The Buildings of Scotland' series) (2006), Yale University Press, London, p.511
92 *SCA Journal*, Issue 19
93 Nigel J.C. Turnbull, *Gordon Millar of Torwood Castle*, unpublished essay, 2010
94 Parris, *A Castle in Spain*, p.164
95 Diana Appleyard, 'Will the last laird please stand up?', 20 January 2007, *Daily Mail*
96 Helen Davies, 'Small castle, big hassle', *The Sunday Times*, 19 January 2003

Chapter 8

97   Walker in *Clow*, p.29
98   Coyne in *Clow*, p.69
99   Walker in *Fawcett and Rutherford Renewed Life for Scottish Castles*, p.167
100 Laing, p.87
101 *Ibid.*, pp.120–1
102 *Ibid.*, p.121
103 Coyne in *Clow*, pp.69
104 James Charles Roy, *The Fields of Athenry*, p. 125
105 Dean and Miers, *Scotland's Endangered Houses*, p.8
106 Walker in *Clow*, p.29

107 Parris, *A Castle in Spain*, p.36
108 Richard Fawcett, *The Conservation of Architectural Ancient Monuments in Scotland: Guidance on Principles*, point 16.1
109 John Ruskin, *The Seven Lamps of Architecture*, p.196
110 Walker in *Clow*, p.29
111 Francis Bacon, 'Of Nobility', *The Essays* (1623), In Officina Ioannis Hauiland, London

BIBLIOGRAPHY

Bailey, Helen, *My Love Affair with Borthwick Castle* (1988), The Book Guild Ltd, Lewes

Bath, Michael, *Renaissance Decorative Painting in Scotland* (2003), National Museums of Scotland

Bevan, Robert, *The Destruction of Memory: Architecture at War* (2006), Reaktion Books, London

Binney, Marcus, Harris, John and Winnington, Emma, *Lost Houses of Scotland* (1980), SAVE Britain's Heritage, London

Browne, Nicholas, *Castles and Crocodiles* (2007), Long John Silver Publishing

Callander, Robin, *How Scotland is Owned* (1998), Canongate Books, Edinburgh

Cantacucino, Sherban and Brandt, Susan, *Saving Old Buildings* (1980), The Architectural Press, London

Clow, Robert (ed.), *Restoring Scotland's Castles* (2000), John Smith & Son, Glasgow

Collins Castles Map of Scotland (1998), Harper Collins, London

Corbett, Judy, *Castles in the Air* (2005), Ebury Press, London

Cormack, Patrick, *Heritage in Danger* (1978), Quartet Books, London

Cornforth, John, *Country Houses in Britain: Can they Survive?* (1974), Woodcote Press, Crawley

Coulson, Charles, *Castles in Medieval Society* (2003), Oxford University Press, Oxford

Coventry, Martin, *The Castles of Scotland* (2006), 4th edition, Birlinn Ltd, Edinburgh

Crook, J.Mordaunt, *The Rise of the Nouveaux Riches* (1999), John Murray, London

Cruden, Stewart, *The Scottish Castle* (1960), Thomas Nelson & Sons Ltd

Dakin, Audrey, Glendinning, Miles and Mackechnie, Aonghus (eds) (2011), *Scotland's Castle Culture*, Birlinn, Edinburgh

Davis, Michael C., *Scots Baronial: Mansions and Castle Restorations in the West of Scotland* (1996), Spindrift Publishing, Ardrishaig

Davis, Michael C., *The Scottish Castle Restoration Debate 1990–2012* (2013), Spindrift Publishing, Ochiltree

Dean, Marcus and Miers, Mary, *Scotland's Endangered Houses* (1990), SAVE Britain's Heritage, London

Devine, T.M. and Finlay, R.J. (eds), *Scotland in the Twentieth Century* (1996), Edinburgh University Press, Edinburgh

Fairbairn, Nicholas, *A Life Is Too Short: Autobiography Vol. 1 (1987),* Quartet Books Ltd, London

Fawcett, Richard, *The Conservation of Architectural Ancient Monuments in Scotland: Guidance on Principles* (2001), Historic Scotland, Edinburgh

Fawcett, Richard and Rutherford, Allan, *Renewed Life for Scottish Castles* (2011), Council for British Archaeology, York

Fenwick, Hubert, *Scottish Baronial Houses* (1986), Robert Hale Ltd, London

Forman, Sheila, *Scottish Country Houses and Castles* (1967), George Outram & Co., Glasgow

Glendinning, Miles, MacInnes, Ranald and MacKechnie, Aonghus, *A History of Scottish Architecture from the Renaissance to the Present Day* (1996), Edinburgh University Press, Edinburgh

Gow, Ian, *Scotland's Lost Houses* (2006), Arum Press, London

Grimble, Ian, *Castles of Scotland* (1987), BBC, London

Hardy, Clive, *Francis Frith's Scottish Castles: Photographic Memories* (1999), Frith Book Company Ltd, Salisbury

Hardy, Matthew (ed.), *The Venice Charter Revisited: Modernism, Conservation and Tradition in the 21st Century* (2009), Cambridge Scholars Publishing, Cambridge

Harris, John, *No Voice from the Hall: Early Memories of a Country House Snooper* (1998), John Murray, London

Harris, John, *Echoing Voices: More memories of a Country House Snooper* (2002), John Murray, London

Hewison, Robert, *The Heritage Industry: Britain in a Climate of Decline* (1987), Methuen, London

Hill, Oliver, *Scottish Castles of the Sixteenth and Seventeenth Centuries* (1953), Country Life Books, London

Historic Scotland, *The Care of Historic Buildings and Monuments in Scotland by Government Departments in Scotland* (1992), Conservation Unit, Department of National Heritage, Edinburgh

Jokilehto, Jukka, *A History of Architectural Conservation* (1999), Elsevier, Oxford

Kelsall, Moultrie R. and Harris, Stuart, *A Future for the Past* (1961), Oliver and Boyd, Edinburgh

Laing, Gerald, *Kinkell: The Reconstruction of a Scottish Castle* (1974), Ardullie House, Dingwall

Liddiard, Robert, *Castles in Context: Power, Symbolism and Landscape, 1066–1500* (2005), Central Books, London

Lindsay, Maurice, *The Castles of Scotland* (1986), Constable, London

Macaulay, Rose, *Pleasure of Ruins* (1953), Walker & Co., New York

MacEwen, John, *Who Owns Scotland?* (1977), EUSPB, Edinburgh

MacGibbon, David and Ross, Thomas, *The Castellated and Domestic Architecture of Scotland from the Twelfth to the Eighteenth Century*, Vols 1–5 (1999), Mercat Press Edinburgh (Facsimile of the edition published by David Douglas, 1887–92). The five volumes can be downloaded in pdf format at: www.electricscotland.com

Maclean-Bristol, Nicholas, *From Clan to Regiment: Six Hundred Years in the Hebrides 1400–2000*, Pen & Sword Books Ltd, Barnsley (included is an account of the restoration of Breachacha Castle)

Macneil of Barra, *Castle in the Sea* (1964), Vintage Press, New York

McCrone, David, Morris, Angela and Kiely, Richard, *Scotland: The Brand* (1995), Edinburgh University Press, Edinburgh

McCrone, David, *Understanding Scotland: The Sociology of a Nation* (2nd edition, 2001), Routledge, Abingdon

McKean, Charles, *The Scottish Chateau: The Country House of Renaissance Scotland* (2001), Sutton Publishing, Stroud

Magnusson, Magnus, *Scotland's Castles and Great Houses* (1981), Weidenfield & Nicolson, London

Queen Marie of Roumania, *The Country That I Love: An Exile's Memories* (Chapter 15: Brana the Beloved) (1925), Duckworth, London

Maxwell, Sir John Stirling, *Shrines and Homes of Scotland* (1938), Alexander MacLehose & Co.

Maxwell-Irving, Alastair M.T., *The Border Towers of Scotland: The West March* (2000), Alastair M.T. Maxwell-Irving, Blairlogie

Melville, Alan, *Castle in the Air: A Comedy* (1951), Samuel French Ltd, London

Miller, Christian, *A Childhood in Scotland* (1989), Canongate Classics, Edinburgh

Montgomery-Massingberd, Hugh and Sykes, Christopher Simon, *Great Houses of Scotland* (2001), Universe

Murdoch, Ken L.S., *Methven Castle: the Restoration of a Seventeenth-Century Building* (2010), Ken L.S. Murdoch, Scotland

Nicolson, Adam, *Restoration: The Rebuilding of Windsor Castle* (1997), Michael Joseph, London

Parris, Matthew, *A Castle in Spain* (revised edition 2012), Penguin Books, London

Pattullo, Nan, *Castles, Houses and Gardens of Scotland*, Vols 1 & 2 (1967), William Blackwood & Sons Ltd, Edinbugh

Peacock, Alan (ed.), *Does the Past Have a Future? The Political Economy of Heritage* (1998), The Institute of Economic Affairs, London

Pendlebury, John, *Conservation in the Age of Consensus* (2009), Routledge, Abingdon

Pratt, Lord Michael, *The Great Country Houses of Central Europe: Czechoslovakia, Hungary, Poland* (1991), Abbeville Press, New York

Rosenberg, Tina Glenapp, *Castle: A Scottish Intrigue* (2009), iUniverse, New York

Roy, James Charles, The Fields of Athenry (2003), Westview Press, Oxford

Ruskin, John, *The Seven Lamps of Architecture* (1889), Sunnyside, London

Saddlemyer, Ann, *Becoming George: The Life of Mrs W. B. Yeats* (2002), Oxford University Press, USA

Salter, Mike, *The Castles of Scotland Series* (5 volumes) (1993–5), Folly Publications, Malvern

Sanderson, Margaret H.B., *A Kindly Place? Living in Sixteenth-Century Scotland* (2002), Tuckwell Press Ltd, East Linton

Scotland's Ancient Heritage (1934), *The Special Summer Number of the SMT Magazine*

Scott-Moncrieff, George, *The Lowlands of Scotland* (1939), B.T. Batsford, London

Simpson, W. Douglas, *Scottish Castles: An Introduction to the Castles of Scotland* (1959), Edinburgh, HMSO

Smith, Dodie, *I Capture the Castle* (1996 edition), Virago, London

Stell, Geoffrey, *Castle Tioram: A Statement of Cultural Significance* (August 2006) Historic Scotland, Edinburgh

Stevenson, Jane, 'Light My Fire' in the collection of three novellas: *Good Women* (2006), Vintage, London

Stokstad, Marilyn, *Medieval Castles* (2005), Greenwood Press, Westport, Connecticut

Strong, Roy, The Roy Strong Diaries 1967–87

Strong, Roy, Binney, Marcus and Harris, John, *The Destruction of the Country House* (1974), Thames & Hudson

Sweetman, David, *Irish Castles and Fortified Houses* (1995), Town House and Country House, Dublin

Tabraham, Christopher, *Scotland's Castles* (1997), Historic Scotland, Edinburgh
———, *Scottish Castles and Fortifications* (1986), The Stationery Office, Edinburgh

Taylor, Robert R., *The Castles of The Rhine: Recreating the Middle Ages in Modern Germany* (1999), Wilfred Laurier University Press, Ontario, Canada

Thurley, Simon, *Lost Buildings of Britain* (2004), Penguin Books, London

Tranter, Nigel, *The Fortified House in Scotland*, Vols 1–5 (1965), Mercat Press, Edinburgh

Charles, Prince of Wales, *A Vision of Britain: A Personal View of Architecture* (1989), Doubleday, London

Walker, David, 'The Architecture of MacGibbon and Ross: The Background to the Books' in Breeze, David, J. (ed.), *Studies in Scottish Antiquity* (1984), John Donald Publishers Ltd, Edinburgh, pp.391–459

Waterson, Merlin, *The Country House Remembered* (1985), Routledge, London

Waugh, Evelyn, *Brideshead Revisited* (2000 edition), Penguin Books, Harmondsworth

Wightman, Andy, *Who Owns Scotland* (1996), Canongate, Edinburgh

Wilkinson, Philip, *Restoration: Discovering Britain's Hidden Architectural Treasures* (2003), Headline Book Publishing, London

Wilkinson, Philip, *Restoration: The Story Continues* (2004), English Heritage, London

Wodehouse, P.G., *Ring for Jeeves* (1999 edition), Penguin Books

Woodward, Christopher, *In Ruins* (2002), Vintage, London

Wright, Patrick, *On Living in an Old Country: The National Past in Contemporary Britain* (1985), Verso, London

Zeune, Joachim, *The Last Scottish Castles* (1992), Verlag, Marie L., Leidorf

Ziolkowski, Theodore, *The View from the Tower: Origins of an Antimodernist Image* (1998), Princeton University Press, Princeton

INDEX